THE CLASSIC ALBUM SERIES

THE STRANGLERS

RATTUS NORVEGICUS AND NO MORE HEROES

by Chris Wade

Classic Album Series: The Stranglers
by Chris Wade

Wisdom Twins Books, 2022
wisdomtwinsbooks.weebly.com

Text Copyright of Chris Wade, 2022

All rights reserved. No part of this publication may be reproduced, stored in a retrieval system, or transmitted in any form or by any means, electronic, mechanical, photocopy, recording or otherwise, without prior written permission of the copyright owner. Nor can it be circulated in any form of binding or cover other than that in which it is published and without similar condition including this condition being imposed on a subsequent purchaser.

THE CLASSIC ALBUM SERIES
THE STRANGLERS

JJ Burnel, bassist for The Stranglers...

CONTENTS

Introduction

The Early Years of The Stranglers

An Interview with Barry Cain

Rattus Norvegicus

An Interview with Martin Rushent

No More Heroes

After Punk

About Chris Wade

Hugh Cornwell and JJ Burnel on Top of the Pops, 1977

INTRODUCTION

This mini book covers the genesis, making, and legacy of two firm punk/new wave classics, Rattus Norvegicus and No More Heroes. Both were recorded and released at the height of the punk rock craze in 1977, and both were made by The Stranglers, the true outsiders of punk, the dirty old men of the new wave. Though the history books have not been kind to The Stranglers, time itself definitely has. Their music is just as powerful and gutsy as ever, their musical brew packing the same punch I am sure it did back in 1977 when they arrived on the scene. They were the most musically proficient of the UK punks by far, and though musical talent wasn't exactly rewarded within the punk scene, for what it's worth The Stranglers could really play. Their sound was like no other, both commercially appealing and at times avant garde. The swirling organs of Dave Greenfield were complimented by JJ Burnel's savage bass lines, Hugh Cornwell's menacing vocals and scratchy, clawing guitars, while Jet Black kept it all in place with his solid, ever reliable back beat. It's a classic sound, and it hasn't aged at all.

The material in this book was first made available in Hound Dawg Magazine, released back at the end of 2009. But I thought it was a nice idea to put it in book form. Here, I examine the two landmark records, when punk rock troubled the charts and kidnapping journalists was just seen as mischievous fun. Join me on a journey back to 77, with The Stranglers as our subject of choice.

Thanks to Barry Cain, Alan Edwards and Martin Rushent, who spoke to me about The Stranglers.

THE EARLY YEARS OF THE STRANGLERS

"Nobody wanted The Stranglers!"
-Ian Grant

Brian Duffy was clearly having what is commonly known as a mid life crisis. Married and with several successful businesses to his name, it clearly wasn't enough for him anymore. In 1973, at the age of 35, he owned a fleet of ice cream vans and an off license situated in Guildford; he was also married to his second wife Helena. Having previously been a jazz drummer as far back as the 1950s, Duffy had always had a fondness for the instrument and was keen to return to the old skins one day. In his younger years he had dabbled with the piano and the violin before moving on to drums. He had some minor success on the cabaret and jazz scene of the 50s, at one point even drumming for Julie Andrews' mum, Barbara, who lived nearby in Walton on Thames. Although he was into the jazzier style, Jet recalls the moment he first heard rock and roll on the radio. For the youth it was exciting, but Jet's dad, like most parents at that time, hated this noisy new craze. He was often heard yelling out, "Turn that racket down!" By the early 70s, a predictable existence in business had ensued, but in the autumn of his years he had had enough of married life and decided to start a band.

"I thought, there has to be something better than this! Let's have another look at that. That's why I decided to start a band."

At first he drummed for the odd group here and there but felt no real mental or creative connection to any of the musicians he encountered. His offbeat ideas obviously needed more off beat people to bounce around with. Here was a middle aged man, clear to the fact that he was going against conventions by even considering a serious career in music at his age, given the fact most pop stars were in their early 20s when they made it. He would search for almost a year before he found the perfect partner to match his musical interests.

Coming over from Sweden with two American draft dodgers and a Swede was one Hugh Cornwell, a biochemistry graduate and musician who was desperate to get his group, Johnny Sox, off the ground but was having little success. His guitar style was quirky and his manners were odd; a true English eccentric. Perfect.

Hugh was born in Kentish town in 1949 to a middle class family. He attended William Ellis School where he had befriended a certain Richard Thompson, future founder of folk rockers Fairport Convention. "Even then he was amazing on the guitar," Hugh said. Thompson taught Hugh how to play bass for their band, Emile and the Detectives. They played a few gigs, perhaps most impressively supporting Helen Shapiro. But when Hugh stayed on for his A levels, Richard left school and went off to form the legendary Fairport Convention. They lost touch with each other and have only recently met up again, some 40 years later.

His early musical interests were in the many eclectic styles echoing around his childhood home; a dad into classical and a brother into jazz. As a teenager Hugh would often sneak out to the Marquee, the legendary London venue, taking in such great acts as the Yardbirds; a mixed palette of musical consciousness indeed and perhaps a part of the reason he became so musically off beat in his later styles. While at Bristol University, where he was studying Biochemistry, Hugh often busked with his acoustic guitar, playing renditions of Beatles and Hendrix tracks. He even played in Keith Floyd's restaurants for a while, beginning a great friendship with the late, wine loving TV legend. It was upon graduating that Hugh went to Lund University in Sweden to fill out a research post and where his interest in Biochemistry soon began to dim in favour of music. He formed a band, Johnny Sox and played various Swedish festivals. While in Sweden, Hugh had befriended a bank robber named Kai Hanson, who was the band's "fairy god mother" like figure; not only did he give them stolen notes to fill up their tank, he also gave them their tour van in the first place. It seems that hints of danger and notoriety were around Hugh well before the formation of The Stranglers. The band was at this point called Johnny Sox, but over the next couple of years this group would slowly mutate into The Stranglers. When Hugh and the band came over to England they met up with the ambitious Brian Duffy, now calling himself Jet Black, who auditioned for Johnny Sox.

"I went to this audition, which turned out to be a squat in Camden Town.," recalled Jet. "Their drummer had quit and I did a rehearsal. I said 'why don't you come and live down in Guildford with me? I have got this huge building, I can put you all up, we got rehearsal rooms and stuff'. It was only when I said I had an off license that they agreed that it would be a good idea to move to Guildford. After two weeks it became obvious no one in the band had any real ambition at all except for Hugh." Jet liked the spirit of the group but admitted their distinct lack of professionalism as a unit was a problem. But he was more than inspired and excited by Hugh's energy, enthusiasm and ambition for music. They got on like a house on fire. Although Jet was a fair bit older than Hugh, the two of them had much in common and shared a quirky interest in their musical outlook and sense of humour. They began jamming together as a unit, but it was becoming clear that the other band members were feeling alienated by Jet and Hugh's obvious closeness. Hugh has said their original goal was to get in on the burgeoning pub rock scene, a plan he shared with Jet.

In typically tongue in cheek fashion, Hugh recalled the line up formation in Zig Zag Magazine.

"It happened by accident. There was this band that came from Sweden, who shall be nameless. They were a four piece which included two American deserters, one Swedish national and an English deserter. We came across to Britain to do pub gigs but blew them out because they weren't any good. Well, the drummer got draft-dodging blues and split back to Sweden, then this amazing piece of flesh here (pointing to Jet Black) said 'Come down to Guilford and rehearse, and we'll get it really good'. So the band moved down to Guilford – the Swedish national, the American deserter and me – and started rehearsing with Jet. It was taking months getting it together and they didn't realise the amount of time it takes to get started. They suddenly realised maybe they should be getting into better things and split, leaving me and Jet with a place to live and a rehearsal room".

One day, before taking off back to his homeland, draft dodging Chicago Mike had hitched a ride from a paint truck driver, a young man with a shaved head and a baby face. His name was JJ. Burnel.

JJ Burnel: "Well, I was coming back from karate, which has been and remains my lifelong passion. I was in my van driving along the old A3 in Kingston and I stopped to give this long-haired, American guy a lift to Guildford. He happened to be the lead singer of a band, who'd come over from Sweden with a few other guys. They were living above this off licence, owned by Jet Black. Jet had then become their drummer and had moved everyone into his off licence. That's how I met Hugh and Jet."

After the draft dodgers returned to the US when Carter gave them amnesty and the Swede returned to live with his family, Hugh and Jet were left alone. It was an odd scenario, but to make matters even stranger, Hugh had moved into the off license where Jet lived with his wife. It was clear Helena was not too happy about having this strange unemployed musician living in their home.

Bored and depressed one day about the lack of progress with the band, Hugh paid JJ a visit. He had his address, so he took round a bottle of wine and as the two men got drunker, Hugh asked JJ if he would be interested in joining the band with him and Jet. Although he could play classical guitar, JJ had never considered a serious musical career; in fact he wanted to move to the USA to become a Harley Davidson mechanic and had an avid interest in Karate, planning eventually to go to Japan to obtain his black belt in the sport. Hugh: "I said, 'Stick with me kid and you'll be able to buy your own Harley Davidson.' Then he left his job and broke his arm in karate when he turned up, which wasn't a very good start. Then we started rehearsing like mad in this scout hut outside Guildford."

Born to French restaurateur parents in Notting Hill, 1952, Jean Jacques had grown into a defensive, aggressive young adult after being bullied at school, hence his eventual fondness for the art of self defence. As a teen he changed his name to John, as to avoid the inevitable prejudice that would be garnered by his French heritage. At school he was a member of the debating society, The British League of Youth, ruffling the feathers of his teachers and being labelled a trouble causer. School friend Brian Crook recalled JJ's rebellious nature, recounting an incident that could have come right out of Lindsay Anderson's If.., when JJ broke into the school weaponry department and held two people up at gun point. He was an outsider, a loner; generally what The Stranglers were to become in their years at the forefront of popular music.

JJ and Hugh instantly connected as friends. "We were like brothers," JJ has since said. "Hugh was a few years older than me and I looked up to him, and he taught me a lot of things. He was more worldly than me, and musically more advanced." It has been documented that during the most rebellious phase of his teenage years JJ was involved with the Hells Angels in Kingston on Thames. His handiness in the field of karate meant he was definitely capable of backing up his words. Hugh on the other hand was not violent as such but had a wicked way with words. Together they formed the confrontational core of the notorious Stranglers that would dominate the pop charts in just under three year's time.

Quite soon JJ had moved into the off license too. Seeing as there wasn't much going on with the band, Hugh and JJ took their time in helping out Jet with his business; selling ice cream down by the river, setting the van up near schools and working behind the counter in the off license. As they made use of themselves in the work environment, they took every opportunity to jam. Jet claims he was the only responsible one out of the three, something of a dad like figure to the two mischievous boys, JJ and Hugh. Can't you just picture it?

"It was a very strange existence, selling ice cream and wine and playing in a band at the same time." Hugh later said. "It was just disillusionment with what we were hearing. We thought nothing's happening in music, there's no excitement anymore. So we thought we could do better ourselves."

Hugh sold JJ his Fender bass and before too long Burnel was mastering the instrument. The fact he was classically trained may explain his rather unique approach to the bass; he plays it like no other with great complexity and aggression. He is utterly one off. The three of them, when any chance arose, would spend hours jamming in the spare room, or at the scout hut, getting a tight rhythm section going. They were now calling themselves Wander Lust, a name which, thank god, would not last too long. Hugh recalls him and JJ listening to The Velvet Underground and rolling joints to Pink Floyd, or sitting in the garden as JJ played classical guitar on sunny days. Although the band was getting well oiled, they knew an extra instrument was required to pad out their minimal sound. Hugh remembered a musician he had known from Johnny Sox in Sweden by the name of Hans Warmling. Excited, Hugh called Hans and asked him if he wanted to come over and join his new band. He agreed and a few weeks later, Mr Warmling was also living in the off license. Warmling had been a member of the band The Jackie Fountains and the semi famous, Sputniks, and was quite a song writer in his own right. When in Johnny Sox, Hans had written some 500 songs and Hugh, always an expert with words, wrote English lyrics to accompany these fine musical pieces. Hugh has called Hans his inspiration and the man who really made him believe he could pursue a musical career.

In Guildford, now with the band line up consisting of Hugh Cornwell on guitar and vocals, JJ Burnel on the bass, Jet Black on drums and Hans Warmling on guitar, sax and keyboards, they took a similar route to mastering their output. Although much of their set was made up of covers, Hans and Hugh worked on a few numbers together. The most notable ones from this period are Chinatown (a cinematic instrumental), My Young Dreams (later to be re recorded by Marriage of Convenience which featured Jet on drums) and the legendary Strange Little Girl (a later top ten hit for the band in 1982). The band's first demo containing these tracks, which was sent round and rejected from every label in London, was recorded at TW Studios in 1974, the very same studio the band recorded their first two albums at. But at the time of their early recording session it was a basic, badly equipped studio, and a far cry from the fairly high production quality it had reached by 1977.

Hans is kind of forgotten by most part time Strangler's fans and only real avid researchers will be aware of his existence.

"Just like there is a forgotten Beatle, there is a forgotten Strangler," Jet said. "He was stunning technically, easily the best musician in the band. We had gone through a few different musicians to try and get something we thought worked and one of these people was Hans. He only worked with us for 6 months. He was one of these rare people who lived and breathed music 24 hours a day."

Around 1975, the band began gigging regularly, with mostly nightmarish results. It seemed no one was digging what they were doing.

"People's reactions were very polarised. Our first gig was in the middle of East Anglia and our soundman got attacked by a middle aged woman with a handbag," said Hugh. "She said we were disgusting. She said 'turn them off!' Even from the very start we have had people fanatically for us and fanatically against us. But we like it like that."

In close agreement JJ recalled the band's first gig being in London, or just outside it. "It was marred by violence. Our mixer was attacked."

It was near enough standard rock music at this point but the band all believed in what they were doing, determined to be successful. Looking back, the band recalls their style and format noticeably different to the current trends of that time. The band themselves also looked very dissimilar to everyone else on the scene, especially Jet who at this point apparently had blonde peroxide hair. Even though they were carving the rugged start of an image, they still had not agreed on a proper name. After a rather unsatisfactory gig one night, JJ calmly sighed, "well the Stranglers have really done it this time." The name The Stranglers started off as a kind of joke, but it began to stick with them. At first, when Hans was still in the group, they were known as The Guildford Stranglers, later to be shortened down to The Stranglers.

Also, while Hans was still around, the band had recorded a demo for a reggae label called Safari Records. The three songs on it, Wasted, My Young Dreams and Strange Little Girl, sound nothing

17

like the Stranglers material that began to grow more aggressive in late 1976, but the demo still has a certain melodic edge and charm. The head of the label, Reg McLean, paid for the recordings and even convinced Hugh and JJ to rent out their rather battered PA system to other acts. Occasionally they would drive the speakers and mixing deck down town to be used by a black girl group. Often finding themselves the only white people at these gigs, Hugh and JJ soon settled in with the "smoky air" and the chilled atmosphere of the black community. "We had been listening to reggae all night," said Hugh, "So Peaches was our attempt at that."

However, the record label who had promised the band a hit single release with My Young Dreams, which was picked as the stand out track, proved to be far from credible. Reg had recorded the songs and then had no intention of ever doing anything with them. He would get a band to sign a contract, do nothing with their demos and then make a cheap buck when a proper label came along wanting to sign them. The band managed to slither out of the contract by pretending to have split up, but this brief taste of possible success being shattered right before their eyes really damaged the group's spirit. But quite soon, they would be getting rather used to constant defeat and disappointment.

By now, Hans was growing increasingly frustrated with the band's live set, which was mostly made up of cover versions. There was a tongue in cheek version of the David Gates hit, If which was recited by Jet in the style that Telly Savalas had scored a hit with it (why oh why isn't there a recording this out there?). The Beatles and old rock n roll numbers were acceptable, but one song just pissed Hans off too much.

"That's why Hans left," said Hugh, "Tie a Yellow Ribbon was the straw that broke his back. There are a lot of chords in it, about 40 or 50. Major sevenths, diminished ninths. He just couldn't be bothered to learn them all. 'We have better songs than this, Hugh, why are we playing this?' He was absolutely right."

Hans left the band, funnily enough, on the way to a gig at a bar mitzvah. Quite simply he told them to stop the ice cream van (now used as the band's tour bus) and when they did so, stepped out of their lives forever. That was it. Hugh didn't meet Hans again until years later, saying he seemed sad and bitter at the band's subsequent success without him. He died tragically in 1995 in a boating accident.

KEYBOARD/ VOCAL MAN FOR SOFT ROCK BAND

That was exactly how the advertisement in the Melody Maker appeared. It also stated: "Mostly original material. Good gear essential. Accommodation available." The band had been playing as a three piece for a while and agreed that a fourth instrument was once again required to fill out their tight rhythm section now that Hans was gone. The advert attracted a whole bunch of hopefuls; a full time sax player apparently named Igor (????) was even tried out to little success. As soon as Dave Greenfield walked into the room though the strange and dynamic atmosphere was instantly apparent. Jet said Dave looked like a hippy, with long hair and a moustache. But physical prejudice aside, this odd looking keyboardist proved to be extremely talented, as they ran through all their standard numbers, including Hanging Around, to tremendous results. "He was so right for the band," Jet said. Dave recalls speaking to Jet on the phone prior to meeting up with him, asking the drummer why they called him Jet. The reply was "Because I'm the fattest thing on two legs."

"Then I met him," Dave laughed "and I thought 'wait a minute. Is everything going to be this odd?' But no, it worked fine." He had trouble finding the place at first and actually had a friend give him a lift to the audition as he didn't have a car at that time. Dave admits his initial thoughts were that these were three very strong, different characters, and wasn't too sure if he could work with them. "You never know till you try."

Dave was born in Brighton in 1949; his early musical interests were in classical guitar and piano, which he taught himself. In his late teens he began touring with countless, since forgotten bands, in army bases and all over the German club scene. He had been in the "almost successful" Rusty Butler at one point, and was growing increasingly frustrated by every band he was involved with either splitting or dissolving. When he joined the Stranglers though, it is certainly clear he lent them much of his musical mastery to their bare three piece sound. Dave's swirling keyboard sound really enhanced the band's general feel, and it was here their comparisons to The Doors began. "No, I have never listened to The Doors," Dave once said, somewhat defensively. To me the comparison to Manzarek is rather irritating, and it is certainly clear that Greenfield was more of a John Lord fan, he being the man who lent Deep Purple their most interesting musical aspect. Now the band had grown somewhat more psychedelic than before and Greenfield's baroque stylings had clearly made the group more interesting. His surreal organ touches and electric piano solos wonderfully played against Hugh's bendy, awkward guitar style. "He was very good at embellishing things," said Hugh. "A lot of it was trade off between keyboards and guitar." All the while Burnel's savage bass lines added extra meat alongside Jet's thundering percussion. They had started to create a sound that was totally original.

JJ remembers the impact Dave had on the band. "Jet and Hugh loved The Beatles but I didn't. I was spending all my time trying to master the bass. When Dave joined he brought a darker side in with his gothic organ and I could identify more with that and we began to get a direction." As a unit, they were now four very different characters creating the strangest sounding music one could imagine, four eccentric poles colliding together in the middle to mutate into the trademark Stranglers sound. From the start The Stranglers agreed on a democratic system, where all song writing credits would be shared equally. This way, the running of the group would flow smoother and all men were equal.

Dave was accepted into the band on a Monday and they played their first gig with him at Wakefield Festival on the Friday (according to Dave's recollections), so it seems he was sort of pushed in at the deep end. Now Reg McLean was out of the picture, the band were keen to get gig work through Savage-Ayris, a small company run by Derek Savage, who would be able to get the band bookings in and around London. But the company had little interest in the group, not seeing great potential in them. At this point Brian Crook, a friend of the band, was in charge as a part time manager; but juggling both his full time job and band commitments proved too difficult for him in the end.

It was when Dave joined, and when the gigs grew more frequent (a reported 3 out of every 4 nights) that the band started to garner a small, though loyal, fan base. Of course their first gig at the legendary Hope and Anchor consisted of one lonesome punter. Apparently, JJ got the chap a chair and the band proceeded to play their whole set to him. He loved it and the following week he brought a few of his friends. "It kind of built from there," said JJ.

Bob Simmons of XL5 recalled a memory of a band that could have been: "In 1976, I was a good friend of Dave Greenfield's and asked him about starting a group. But he told me he'd joined a group called the Stranglers and they had a year's worth of gigs lined up. Because I couldn't get him as a keyboard player, we basically formed a guitar band." Unlucky.

In late 1975 the group gained residencies at the Hope and Anchor in Islington and The London Red Cow. The band's set list was growing more like what is commonly known as classic Stranglers material. An early fan was Garry Coward Williams, nicknamed Chiswick Charlie by Hugh, who took some of the first ever photos of the band. Another was Charles Edwards who had the honour of having a song written about him by The Stranglers, called Charlie Boy. A very rough demo of this track exists and it is a shame, suggesting from the degraded format, that it never got into the proper Stranglers set, as it's a charming little number with a nice melody. There are other songs from this era which are particularly worth tracking down on bootlegs. I Know It is a typically 70s upbeat rocker featuring a fine Hugh vocal and a cool groove. JJ sings the catchy Make You Mine, and it is in these songs we hear a hint of classic Stranglers, although this particular song was dropped after Hans departed (who incidentally provides the song with a neat harmonica solo.) By this point though the songs were reshaping and the band were getting good at penning catchy numbers. Hanging Around, Tomorrow was the Hereafter (soon dropped but rereleased as a freebie by the Stranglers fan club in 1980), Bitching and Get a Grip, among others, were emerging now faster, more upbeat and certainly more aggressive.

Hugh has said on many occasions that the aggression in their music had come about by frustration, not only frustration that their music was getting mostly negative reactions but also the fact they were all so poor, with a far from ideal way of living. Jet's businesses were not doing so well now and he was slowly selling them off. It was around this time that he and his wife separated.

Shane Rawlinson recalled a friend of his who had a job ejecting squatters from houses. He recalled going to one house in Chiddingfold, where he was told a rock band were squatting. He went inside and saw mattresses and used needles scattered about the floor. Whether this was The Stranglers or not we'll never know.

The band were now relocated to a house in Chiddingfold as mentioned, this being the basis for another one of the group's ill fated names. Jet, speaking in 1995, explains: "We were first called The Chiddingfold Chokers which was an in-house joke in those early days. Eventually we ended up with the name the Stranglers in desperation because we couldn't think of something we all agreed on. We were sitting round one week writing songs and watching the odd movie on TV and every movie seemed to have a strangling in it. The name was a colossal problem in the early days. When we were ringing up venues to get a gig they'd ask us what we were called and we'd say The Stranglers and you could hear them creasing on the other end or slamming the phone down. It was a bit of a handicap, it still is a bit of a handicap in some countries."

Incidentally, when approaching pubs and venues for gigs by telephone, Hugh would enquire what kind of music they put on at their establishment. If the answer was that they only put on "country and western", Jet would ring up a couple of days later saying "we're a country band." Of course, when The Stranglers set up and began to play their unique brand of sweaty pub rock, the venue owners were far from delighted.

To make matters worse, in Chiddingfold the band were so poor that they rarely had enough money to get a decent meal. JJ was once left alone in the house for two days with no money and no food. The only option was to walk five miles down the road to pick some tomatoes that were growing right beside a sewage farm. Desperate times indeed. Hugh explains; "We were sometimes so poor that all we had was enough money to go to the pub and buy some mixed nuts and a couple of pints of Guinness." It was the hard times that inspired the lyrics to the band's first hit single Get a Grip on Yourself. "It was like a prison sentence," Hugh said. Jet summed up this far from hopeful period. "Times were hard. It took a lot of hard work. Sometimes it looked as if we wouldn't make it until the end of the week."

But Jet was keen to explain that even though the band were poor and going down like a lead balloon as a live act, they were still enjoying themselves. "We were having a whale of a time, yeah; it was a lot of fun, like a big endless party for nearly three years. We didn't get paid and we were broke and we were skint and we were starving, but we were still having a good time, funnily enough. At least that's how I remember it."

If the gigs were far from well received it may have had something to do with the ridiculousness of the chosen venues. One gig was in Purley at the Conservatives club. Hugh remembered this occasion not so fondly:

"375 people walked out on us at that gig. They all turned up in ultra-smart evening dress and as soon as we started they began drifting out. By the time we'd finished there were about three people left! Right in the middle of a number a guy came up and grabbed me. I thought he was going to get heavy, but he just launched into a very intellectual rap about why we weren't working with the audience, the ethnic quality of the music and bluurrggh!. We just told him to piss off and kicked him off the stage". Seeing all these people getting so offended and alienated by their music helped The Stranglers in a special way to fully understand what they were doing and what they represented. "Here was an audience we could see didnt have the perception and the interest in music to even want to listen to us. It is often very easy to assess what an audience reaction will be by the way they look. So that was pretty cool."

Another gig had the band booked as a quick replacement for the Ian Gillian Band at Glasgow University. "We'd gone up in the ice cream van," JJ recalled "and the people were not happy. They wanted to tear us apart." Radio producer Stewart Cruickshank recalled the gig as "a phenomenal punk rock performance," also noting that JJ Burnel was "karate-ing people off the stage!" The band had to barricade themselves into a dressing room to escape the angry mob, who were clearly disappointed at having to sit through The

Stranglers rather than The Ian Gillian Band! The fools! The band quickly rushed their gear into the ice cream van and escaped from Glasgow, amazingly, without harm. Other ridiculous gigs were supporting Ricky Valance to twelve people and playing, of all places, at a Convent!

The band rarely went down well and each gig was as disastrous as the last. "We frequently didn't get paid or we were told to get out if we didn't play something they knew. People used to throw tables at us," remembered Jet.

Derek Savage had now formed the Albion agency with Dai Davies, the office of which was situated above a ladies hairdressers in Putney of all places. "It stunk awful of perm chemicals as you walked in," said Hugh. The Stranglers began asking the pair of them for representation, but initially Savage saw little potential in the band. After Hugh's nonstop bombardment of pestering and insistence that they sign them (which included a weekly cartoon comic strip that Hugh drew, making the two of them out to be lazy gits in their office) they agreed to help out these four strange individuals calling themselves The Stranglers. Hugh said the character of the Stranglers appealed to Albion. "They thought we were entertaining; with the ice cream van Jet was quite a character. A bizarre collection of people you wouldn't get in a room together if we weren't in a band together." In October 75 Ian Grant was brought in to take over the case and invest more time in the band. Grant had some prior experience as an agent and Crook, though a loyal friend and of great assistance, could not really put in full time efforts for the band. The first time Grant saw the band live they were supporting Viv Stanshall (ex Bonzo Dog Doo Dah Band) at the Nashville. "The songs were ridiculously catchy," said Grant. Seeing as the record companies were showing little or no interest in the band's demos, Albion were sure the best thing to do now was get The Stranglers as many gigs as possible all over the country.

Chas De Whalley, in the NME, had given the band a favourable mention, referring to their performance at the Hope and Anchor in September 1975. Albion were so pleased with De Whalley's favourable words that they asked him to write a promotional hand out for the band. It was here that the mention of the word PUNK first became associated with The Stranglers.

To accompany their plans, Ian Grant also had the ingenious idea of assigning a top publicist to brand the Stranglers in the press and create a public persona. Alan Edwards was right for the job; he had freelanced for Record Mirror and worked for top publicist Keith Althman, representing T Rex and The Who, among others.

Hugh and the band were all on the dole by now, with no money from the gigs coming in. They loved playing music and wouldn't give it up for the world, but frankly they were getting nowhere. Warned by the DHSS that he HAD to look for work, Hugh got the paper and applied for a job as an A Level biology teacher for kids who had been ejected from regular schooling. Of course the stuffiness and day to day, 9 to 5 boredom of the job depressed Hugh and made him even more determined to succeed in music. Before too long he had been sacked from his role at the school for wearing jeans to work and drinking at the pub with some of his pupils. The place was run by Mrs Hobbs, a stuck up "ogress" according to Hugh. The song School Mam, which eventually appeared as the closer on No More Heroes was based on a fantasy situation Hugh thought up involving Hobbs catching a teacher having sex with his pupils. As this woman was so sexually repressed, and had never seen anyone having sex before, she climaxes at the sight of the teacher's frolicking and dies "with contentment on her wrinkled old face ever more." The song, easily one of the most shocking of their live set, was made even more outrageous with a stage antic Hugh began to do in 1976. Hugh would pretend to masturbate his throat and then proceed to "ejaculate" all over the crowd with his saliva. So with this dramatic wank it may be Hugh who inspired the whole punk gobbing phenomenon. "Sorry everyone," Hugh later said in his defence.

FILE UNDER PUNK ROCK

"WE were the Godfathers of punk!"
-Jet Black

Jet Black: "Well, we wanted to do our kind of music, which is a bit offbeat when one looks at current trends. We didn't want to follow everybody else and we have stuck to that. In the early days the criticism was pretty horrendous! Now people realise we are refreshingly different and that's what we wanna stick to".

Imagine yourself sat in the crowd at an early Stranglers gig, at the Red Cow, the Hope and Anchor or the Nashville. There on the stage are a group of ragged outcast misfits firing out the weirdest, most aggressive music you have ever heard; shouting, swearing and basically looking old enough to know better. Look to your left and you may see a long haired pre Sex Pistols John Lydon, or a young pre Clash Joe Strummer. If The Stranglers weren't fully a punk band (the phrase hadn't yet been associated with them) then why did their style and attitude so strongly influence a lot of the future bands who were key to the public's perception of punk rock? Could it be that Mr Rotten and Mr Strummer decided not to admit the truth that these guys pre-dated their own highly celebrated bands? The attitude of The Stranglers was punk for sure, but the fashion element, well that was accidental. "They adopted the safety pin as a fashion prop, but our attire was degraded through poverty. I think people took it up as a fashion," Jet Black later said.

"I don't think we were punks at all," said Dave. "They can call me an old punk now, fine, I know I wasn't."

Hugh recalls the difficulties of remaining a part of the punk in crowd amidst the wave of bands coming in. "It was very hard to remain a separate identity at that time. All these bands were coming to see us before they even started playing at the Red Cow and Hope and Anchor. In fact Chrissie Hynde offered to be our singer. It was a nice offer but there wasn't any room really."

The band stuck out for a number of reasons; the fact they were older, especially Jet Black, who was double the age of the average punk rocker. JJ once joked to the NME about Jet's age, saying "It's closer to four digits than three." Jet looked wise, rather like an aging owl and was the furthest from a snotty little punk rocker as you could get. Also the keyboard element, which was so unhip, separated them from the other bands. Sonically they sounded much more menacing, powerful and musically layered than the others. The Pistols were loud I'm sure and much of their shock reaction was down to this, but The Stranglers had the real musical class.

As far as fitting in to the punk surroundings, JJ has said, "There were very few places for guys with short hair and leather jackets to hang out. So the only other people we could hang out with were the punks."

Hugh thinks the fact the group didn't fit in with the others had something to do with their success.: "Because we missed that pub rock thing — we were too young and not good enough to be a part of it— the pub rock musicians sneered at us. And then when the punk thing happened we were too good and too old. So we were this misanthropic group between the two. And that stayed with us. We were a class of one. But it didn't stop our success."

As 1976 progressed, the band began to garner a small following of loyal fans. A regular and soon to be close friend was a certain Dagenham Dave. Originally from Manchester, he was an honest half caste man from a working class background; a self taught man, well read and educated, working as a scaffolder at this point. Hugh had nicknamed him Dagenham Dave because he had once worked at Ford's Dagenham Plant. Chiswick Charlie remembered his first meeting with Dave. "The first time I met him was in the summer of 1976. At that time I was working as The Stranglers road crew. We were playing a gig at the Golden Lion in Fulham and after the gig this guy came up to me while I was putting the gear away. 'Fucking great gig man,' he said. After that brief meeting I got to know him quite well." Though he did have a girlfriend called Brenda, Dave's first love was music. Hugh said that Dave's favourite bands were the Tubes (who Hugh soon got into) and The Stranglers. He loved the band and worshipped them, at one point even offering the lot of them the use of his woman. Having this unknown band to himself certainly appealed to Dave and he was soon coming to every gig he could. The band in turn loved to hang out with this party loving rogue. He really gave them a bit of hope through the hard times and repeatedly insisted they would eventually make the big time. He was right.

It was now that punk rock was taking shape and bands like The Sex Pistols were garnering controversy and outrage in the newspapers and from the music press. The shift began with a general scene which was rebelling against predictable, corporate rock, led by the pub rock bands. But there was a small amount of groups who were just a little bit more aggressive. Dr Feelgood were clearly the forerunners of punk, a group who according to JJ don't get enough credit for influencing the genre. The change in the general appearance and attitude of punters was soon apparent and the Stranglers audience was soon growing more punk by every gig. By that I mean more aggressive, more intense and certainly livelier. Their music was speaking out to a certain element of people, as was the music of the other angry young men on the scene. JJ recalls the Stranglers position in the burgeoning punk rock movement.

"Our management were involved with The Ramones so we started listening to what we were told were our contemporaries. At the same time we were doing gigs and they fucking hated us and we were starting to get aggressive. The pubs that would let us play were attracting a certain type of public and the girls we were shagging were all punkettes. I also got into a lot of fights and looked for trouble. I soon considered the punks a bit wimpy. We were a crossover. More hardcore punks didn't like us and the kids 17/ 18 adopted us as their punk band."

Music promoter Dylan White recalled his experience of seeing the Stranglers in 1976. "We were in the front row and The Stranglers came on stage. My mate rolled a spliff. Hugh Cornwell leant forward and took it. I was pretty impressed with this. The Stranglers tunes just stuck in our brains; things like Sometimes, Dead Ringer, Bitching. They were older, so could they really be punks? But that sort of became irrelevant."

The press were really starting to hype punk as the new shocking force in social and musical rebellion. In a big story for News of the

World, The Stranglers were picked out as the forerunners and the prime example of the genre's shocking and appalling controversy. Hugh was branded "a brainy drop out!" The newspaper seemed to be wondering where Hugh and the band drew inspiration for their shocking songs from. Hugh replied that it was from their experiences. When the News of the World pushed for more revealing glimpses, Hugh defended with "But that's our private lives! It's got nothing to do with the general public". In the same article, when referring to the leather thong he wore around his neck, Hugh joked, "I'll tighten the knot to give me more blood to the head; like a shot of adrenalin." The thrill of the outrage was hard to resist.

In May 76, The Stranglers supported US punk Patti Smith at the London Roundhouse. It was a terrific opportunity for the Stranglers and Albion had done extremely well to get them the gig. Unfortunately for the band, it all went horribly wrong. The crowd were restless in their verbal assault and the band went down terribly. The second night at the Roundhouse the band, once again, just weren't winning over Patti's fans. So, as was always the case when things weren't going smoothly, the band launched into their most offensive piece, the joke number Tits. The track had Hugh introducing each band member individually before the said instrumentalist launched into a deliberately awful solo. It was a piss take, but from then on, Smith's fans actually started to enjoy the show. Several record company A and R men had frequented the gig and none of them were impressed by the Stranglers X rated shenanigans. One of these A and R men was Andrew Lauder of United Artists, whom the Stranglers management had been constantly nagging to sign the band. UA had turned them down on numerous occasions, and the Roundhouse gig did nothing in changing their minds. Still, the scale of the Patti Smith support slot lent the band a considerable amount of kudos and publicity.

Although they weren't accepted as part of the punk scene, Sniffin Glue, the original punk rock fanzine had good words to say about the band in their second issue, released in August 1976. "The group consists of a very straight looking drummer, who keeps a very sound beat throughout; an organist who looks like he's just come home from Woodstock; a bass player who looks like a Ramone and a singer/ guitarist who just looks scruffy. Together they add up to one of the most original groups I've ever seen on the pub circuit."

"One gig I remember," Hugh recalled, "the bill was Ian Dury, supported by The Stranglers and The Sex Pistols. The Pistols were on first; they were just jumping around on stage in these suits that were way too big for them. It was very comical." There were 25 punters in attendance.

However, the divide between the Stranglers and the rest of the punk bands was to get much more serious. One night at Dingwalls club in 1976, when The Stranglers were chosen to support US punk stars The Ramones and The Flamin' Groovies (at a kind of punk bicentennial gig where The Stranglers represented the UK), things came to a head with some notable members of the punk rock scene. JJ Burnel, in a particularly aggressive mood, got into a bit of a scrap with Paul Simenon, bassist with The Clash. Of course this scrap has now gone down in rock history as a legendary moment of typical rock n roll machismo, but it can also be pin pointed as the exact moment that the press and the punk in crowd turned on the Stranglers. Firstly, The Stranglers had been chosen over the two major punk groups, The Clash and the Pistols, to represent England in this very silly punk unity, which had actually taken place firstly at The Roundhouse before the surprise Dingwalls show the following night. Perhaps they were all just a little bit jealous that these four dirty old men had got the most sought after gig of the year so far. But of course none of them would have admitted this. After the show, various members of the punk rock in crowd were hanging around Dingwalls, drinking and chatting. Burnel was feeling slightly light headed after having too much to drink. In those days, Paul Simenon had what he called a nervous tick, which involved him spitting on the ground for no apparent reason. Unfortunately, he happened to let out a gob full of saliva just as a certain Jean Jacques Burnel was walking past him that night. JJ quite simply flipped and smacked the bass player round the chops. Much commotion did follow, with JJ and Paul pressed right up against each other's faces yelling out every insult under the sun. Hugh, calmly enjoying a drink with The Clash front man Joe Strummer, leaned over and said, "I think my bass players having a go at your bass player." The whole commotion ended up outside; two sides opposing one another like a showdown in an old western movie. On one side, members of The Ramones, The Clash and Chrissie Hynde, in other words the hip punk in crowd, and on the other side The Stranglers.

"Me and Paul had a massive punch up," JJ recalled, "And it was in front of everyone, including the press in the courtyard of Dingwalls in London. On one side of the fence there was Dee Dee Ramone and on the other side, the press and other people. We had a punch up and a few noses were out of joint, because we were chosen over The Clash and The Sex Pistols to play with The Ramones. Ever since that the press were against us." Apparently, as the fight raged on, and Dagenham Dave put a certain John Lydon up against a van by his throat, Hugh was sat in the van with a girl. "What should have happened was we should have all had a good night and a few drinks together. I felt like a good night had been sabotaged"

At the time, JJ felt as if he were fighting for a cause, for his band and his reputation, and perhaps he did get off on his tough guy image a bit. But years later, when I met JJ after a gig in Leeds, another fan was asking him about this legendary night outside Dingwalls. JJ, to be honest, seemed bored with the conversation, saying "It was a long time ago, I can't really remember it." Even he has admitted how such reckless behaviour seriously slowed down the bands success and could have ruined them. In the press though, The Stranglers still took every opportunity to alienate themselves from the punk crowd. "The Ramones should stick to playing tennis," said Hugh.

Though The Stranglers would be the first to admit they were playing up to the punk label in order to get more media attention, they weren't the only band to do so. Look at The Jam, the Police and especially Elvis Costello; none of these people were punk, yet the association with the movement helped them along in their pursuit for success and recognition. But although the Stranglers were shrugged off as the least accepted of all the punk bands, they had much more guts than the more recognised groups in terms of real life aggression.

All these years on, JJ has an interesting view on the other punk bands of this era and the bad attitude that they gave off.

"A lot of the punk bands, if you want to call them that, were kind of pretending. There was an attitude, they put the clothes on and suddenly there was a different attitude, they put on an attitude. They weren't sure about us because we were out on a limb compared to the other bands of that period and we seemed to be a bit more the real thing."

It must also be noted that by now The Stranglers were gigging regularly, working hard but living in squalor. In 1976 they played an amazing 191 gigs; they were the real hard workers. But Malcolm McLaren, the man who wanted to create as much hype as possible in his group The Sex Pistols, was holding private gigs for his band, mostly playing to private gatherings of journalists. It was almost like a manufactured group - with spitting. "They were really hyped and had lots of support from the press," said JJ.

Glen Matlock, former Pistol, recalled an incident when he was in the middle of a photo shoot with the band and JJ Burnel sped by on his motorcycle. The two men said hi to one another and continued on their ways. John Lydon, or should I say Johnny Rotten, turned to Matlock and snarled, "You don't talk to people like that do you?"

The band recall Joe Strummer being a friend and admirer before the big media split, at one point even crying on Hugh's shoulder, "I wish I had a band like yours!" But later, he was anti Stranglers. Why is this so? To be fair, Hugh has said that away from the UK Strummer and The Clash were always good mates. Perhaps it was all the press and their evil doings?

Jet also recalls The Pistols' Paul Cook asking him for drum tips after gigs. There may have been a hidden fondness between the bands out of the public eye, as all punk bands looked upon each other with an accepted sense of mutual hatred, but JJ put much of The Stranglers own punk alienation down to the fact that they refused to follow all the silly rules. "For not going down King's Road to the Roebuck and the sex shop," he noted. The Stranglers stand aside from the pretentious side of punk; the hipness and the standard to which a "proper punk" had to set themselves to. It must also be noted that the choice drug for the average punk was speed; Greenfield was most certainly an acid head and JJ loved a puff of the old dope. Hugh was into the lot, but experimented responsively (he claims the key to successful drug taking is to control the drug, not let the drug control you). This further enhanced their image as dirty old hippies. But that said, JJ still relished his role as a punk rocker, very much considering himself part of the movement.

In October 76, they supported US punk star Patti Smith once again for two nights at the Hammersmith Odeon. This was surprising given the hostile reaction the Stranglers had got from Patti's fans in June, but her promoter John Curd liked the band very much and was keen on giving them a second chance. As most agreed, although their set was often full of disastrous events, there was a certain aura around the group that made you want to come back. . Andrew Lauder of UA was there once again after being invited down by Albion for what was one of the Strangler's biggest shows yet. The first night went down superbly, with the band's punky set starting with Grip and finishing with Go Buddy Go, getting thunderous applause from the packed house. Of course, in typical Stranglers bad luck, the second night was a nightmare. Andrew Lauder, once again, was not impressed. But when Albion set up a performance at Fulham studios for Lauder to witness the band in relaxed mode, with no crowd distractions or possible hiccups with unreliable PA systems, he was blown away.

The timing was right and punk was beginning to look like a proper possibility in the scheme of commercial music. Not only was it proving that anyone could start a band, it was also showing that pop music didn't have to be syrupy and commercial. Rules were being altered amidst the mayhem. The Damned had been signed by indi label Stiff Records (the first British punk album of all time) and CBS had signed The Clash. Although neither of these albums were big hits, the established labels definitely saw mega bucks in the possibilities that punk held. They knew that if they played it right they could get as much dosh out of this era as possible, while in the process spending very little money on recording (and paying) the groups in question. On December 6th 1976, The Stranglers signed to United Artists. The publicity that followed was ridiculous, as was the outrage caused by the fact that another nasty punk group had got a record contract. Many "professional" musicians and prog rock superstars just couldn't see the fairness or the validity of signing another group of these "talentless punk rockers." Also the fact it was for 40,000 quid made it all the more outrageous.

While a less responsible band might have gone out and blown their advance payments on drugs or lavish items, The Stranglers invested much of their new found cash into replacing their battered equipment. The same week they got signed, their tour van collapsed, after racking up somewhere close to 80 000 miles. It was just in time.

Not long after the band got signed, a historic event occurred that drastically changed the mood of Stranglers concerts even further. One set of friends who fell for the Stranglers were the now legendary

Finchley Boys, a group of thuggish proto punks with a violent gang mentality and a love for the Stranglers' music. The Finchley Boys all grew up in council estates in London, and all got together well before The Stranglers were building up notoriety on the London music scene. Primarily angry with the world, like much of the youth of that time, the boys were looking for a band who matched their outlook on life; music that spoke to them and for them.

Alan Hillier, one of the most renowned of the Finchley Boys later wrote, "Without exchanging a single word to each other in that little, noisy arena on that momentous night, we realised, collectively, that we were witnessing one of the greatest live bands of our time. The energy they created reflected our own character, our own passion and emphasised our desire. It was exactly what we had been waiting for."

The relationship between the Finchleys and The Stranglers began when the band were playing a gig one night at the Torrington pub in Finchley, and in came a whole bunch of short haired lads looking hard as nails. They quickly filed into the bathroom and emerged several minutes later done up like hardcore punks. The bouncers would never have let them in had they been dressed in their punk garb. In a rush of excitement they invaded the stage. The band, bewildered and worried that a fight may be coming, carried on playing regardless. Much to their surprise, the fierce looking gang began to dance.

JJ spoke of the Finchley Boys regularly, often waxing lyrical about their honesty and reliability. He told the Hanging Around fanzine, "They are a bunch of guys from Finchley who have been with us for about a year now and they have developed into a hardcore elite. They won't take any crap, they are real people. Some of them work for a living, but they don't go around making a big deal about the dole queues because to them it's the worst thing that could happen to them. They are hard working kids and although we don't claim to be working class spokesmen, they respect us and dig us because we try to be straight with them."

Here began the legendary relationship with The Stranglers and their fans. It is hard to think of a more loyal following than theirs; the Stranglers fans have always stuck by them and are always REALLY into what they do, expressing intense interest and honest criticism. In turn the band treat their fans well; with respect and appreciation. PR man Alan Edwards noted the strength of this bond.

"The Stranglers had a genuine and strong bond with their fans, especially the legendary Finchley Boys, who featured a cast of characters from Dennis Price to Lester Purdie. They were as one with their audience and the bond was strong and almost unbreakable."

Original fan Garry Coward Williams didn't exactly warm to the Finchley Boys, clearly disliking what he saw as unnecessarily aggressive behaviour. But aggression was now very much a part of the band's existence, and certainly a key to the driving force of the punk rock boom. Grant often had a considerable amount of trouble trying to get the band gigs due to the unavoidable violence that would take place, but at the same time found the controversy attracted the attention of the news headlines. It was an irresistible though dangerous game.

Dennis Marks, a Finchley Boy leader, recalled the confusion of the time regarding punk rock. "We weren't sure what punk rock was. As it happens we looked like punks at the end of the gig because we'd been ripping each other's clothes. The whole evening was amazing!"

From then on The Finchley Boys were at every show The Stranglers did, or at least every gig they could make. It was a comforting fact for the band to know they had a loyal bunch of handy lads at every gig. But Dagenham Dave, the number one fan, was far from pleased to see these new, unwanted admirers moving in on his turf. Dave liked the punk music but couldn't quite get the people who followed it.

Dave really loved The Stranglers, not only musically but as people too. He would spoil them with booze and drugs after gigs and even put them up for the night if they had nowhere to stay. Something clicked in him one night at the 100 Club when Dave picked a fight with seven or eight of the Finchley Boys during a Stranglers gig. It was a blood bath; and although he put up one hell of a fight, Dave had his skull fractured and his ribs broken in the brawl. The experience left a very sour taste in people's mouths and Dave was a broken man.

When the Stranglers were recording their first album, Rattus Norvegicus, producer Martin Rushent recalled Dave hanging around the studio, trying to tell him how to do his job. He knew how to get the best out of HIS band better than any record producer did!! Unfortunately Brenda got sick of his behaviour and left him. Dave simply couldn't handle it anymore and on the 9th of February 1977, he committed suicide by jumping into the Thames off Tower Bridge. They pulled his body out of the mud about a week later. In tribute, The Stranglers wrote a song for their first big fan. Typically it was far from sentimental, but it was in the fashion Dave would have wanted; pure Stranglers. The real tragedy with Dave's death I suppose is how he never got to see his No. 1 band hit the big time.

By the time the band were signed and the recording of their first record was in discussion, The Stranglers were relishing their new found controversial reputation. The boys loved to shock. JJ told Zig Zag magazine, "We're clean wholesome boys. We're just like the boys next door, if you happen to live next door to a morgue!"

In January, when the band were supporting The Climax Blues Band at the Rainbow, Hugh wore a rather eye catching T shirt on stage with what appeared to be the word FUCK on it. The GLC were in the vicinity, clearly worried about all the controversy this punk rock was now causing. They demanded Hugh remove the offending item or the power would be turned off. In the end, Hugh put the T shirt on back to front, and then, in typically outrageous form, turned his back to the crowd. The plug was pulled. This sort of publicity, though bad, was just what their PR man was looking for. Alan Edwards, the man behind all this branding, certainly was young but he knew what he was doing. He thought it was right to establish The Stranglers as real bad boys, but has since said that he didn't have to exaggerate all that much. "I don't know if Hugh blames me or gives me any credit for helping to pull them towards punk, image wise. Maybe I was pulling them unnaturally into something that wasn't really them but because they were highly intelligent, it was something they soon comprehended and manipulated."

By further enhancing their punk credentials, Edwards started the very punk Stranglers fanzine, Strangled! The magazine began as a crude, DIY style rag and wound up as a glossy item of considerably fascinating content well into the 1990s. Edwards knew the best way to get the band constant exposure was to really hammer home their outrageous manner. He was also the one who first thought up the idea of having JJ as the band's sex symbol and the number one punk pin up.

As a band, and a collective voice, The Stranglers represented something very different to the other punk bands. The Pistols were all about the boredom of everyday life, dole queues and anarchy. The Clash did the whole rock against racism thing, speaking out for causes without ever practising them in real situations. The Stranglers were always the practical, honest ones. They never set out to be spokesmen for any minority, never pretended to be anything but what they actually were; a rock n roll band with an edge. The subject matter of their lyrics was often out of touch with what the other groups in the punk movement were singing about. Apart from a few exceptions (the punk anthem Something Better Change) their songs were about seemingly irrelevant things; like bad acid trips, a little bit of social and urban alienation, ogling women, being in a rock band, pervy teachers, wicked ladies and hanging around gay bars doing nothing in particular. There was very little emphasis on the big issues of politics (apart from where JJ's views of a united Europe began to show prominence in later material). In these early days it was The Stranglers' music which rocked the most out of all their other contemporaries, and the lyrics were much darker, more dangerous and very surreal. This was 60s psychedelic revisited, with more than a hint of 1970s disillusionment. The Stranglers, perhaps, spoke out to the no nonsense rock fan, the unpretentious ones out for a top tune. They represented a middle ground; for those people into the punk ethic of breaking down the barriers, but not so much into the tuneless sounds it often fired out, The Stranglers were the perfect fit. They were proficient, angry enough, but with more than a grasp on a decent melody. This was their crime in the eyes of the punk in crowd, as well as the fact that they would soon be "selling out" by signing to a major label and going on Top of the Pops.

But what was punk? A word and a movement thought up by a small community of press people, that's all. But it turned into a mass phenomenon that for a short while looked as if it could spell the end of law and order in modern Britain. The Stranglers were, no matter what you read in the history books, very much a part of that scene!

Alan Edwards summed up the appeal and contradictions of a truly strange and brilliant band to me;

"The Stranglers were punk's wild bunch. They rode into town and it all went off. No political sloganeering or handbags at dawn, more like battle of the Alamo - every night! Dave Greenfield, a peaceful and genuinely eccentric character, never far from a crossword puzzle and always ready with a wizard keyboard run dripping with psychedelia. He was the resident hippie. Jet, the affable pub landlord type, straightforward bloke; you knew where you were with him. His drumming was straightforward too. He was very much the Ringo providing stability for the other musicians to work off. JJ was an intense, contradictory character and a truly innovative and brilliant bassist to boot..... often literally. His strongly held political views reflected his European background and perspective. Hugh was the slightly detached academic with a great talent for song writing, deserving of more critical acclaim than he received. To achieve chart success with a song that referenced Shakespeare, Trotsky and Lenny was truly the product of a genius, albeit a slightly off the wall one! They were also the odd bunch. Quite how Jet, Hugh, Jean and Dave came to be in the same band is anybody's guess."

JJ explains how four odd individuals may have chanced upon each other; "Just a desire, but otherwise we had nothing in common really with each other. Just a desire to change things for ourselves and also in relation to what was happening musically at the time. We were nowhere - just had nothing in common with the general scene at the time."

INTERVIEW: BARRY CAIN

Barry Cain worked for the Record Mirror in the late 70s and was one of the few Stranglers' champions in the press. He helped organise the infamous Iceland trip when he temporarily worked with Alan Edwards as the band's PR and even transcribed Hugh's prison diary to book form in 1980. His great book, 77 Sulphate Strip, was a detailed glimpse into the year of punk rock, littered with the exciting articles he wrote at the time.

What did you think of them when you first met The Stranglers? Who did you meet first?

Saw them for the first time in Dingwalls, Camden Town, September 1976. They were the first 'punk' band I'd experienced and they blew me away. I hadn't heard music like it before – it opened the cemetery gates and let death into my life. And boy, could they play. I was introduced to Hugh backstage and I convinced myself he was a wind-up merchant. He had the devil in his eyes and I wasn't sure if his smile was painted because there seemed to be something behind it, as Smokey would say. The other three kept themselves to themselves and just gave me a cursory nod. Hugh was the PR man in those dangerous Cambridge rapist days.

What did you think to Rattus when you first heard it, in your original review and looking back how does it stand up now?

The night before the first album chart was released that might feature Rattus, I was in the upstairs bar at the Roundhouse sitting at a table with Julie Burchill, Tony Parsons and a PR from WEA who was totally dismissive of punk and bet us each twenty quid that Rattus wouldn't make the Top Twenty. It debuted at 4 and he sent over the cash to Record Mirror by messenger. Something that good couldn't escape and I couldn't lose. I confess I haven't played Rattus in years – still not as long ago as the last Beatles album I slipped into the machine. But each track is embedded in my heart and when I occasionally hear on TV or radio the opening chords to Peaches, or the verse of Hanging Around or that oft used chunk of Down in the Sewer, my heart skips a beat. Music like that can never date.

A lot of journalists were scared of The Stranglers. Did you consider yourself lucky to always be treated well by them?

I never even thought about it. I was brought up on the 'mean' streets of Kings Cross and The Angel where skinheads roamed like buffalo and boys got murdered. The Stranglers were middle-class in comparison, bulging with university degrees and post adolescent angst. I liked each one of them and perhaps they sensed that. Also, I wrote some blinding reviews, which definitely helps.

Did you make the Iceland Black and White trip in 78, if so how do you remember those chaotic 2 days?

I actually helped to arrange the Iceland trip when I worked briefly as the band's PR alongside Alan Edwards at Modern Publicity. It was four of the strangest days I'd ever known and there's an account of it in my new book, '78 rpm, which should be out early next year. Also included is an on the road piece with the band in Japan in '79 and a mad night in Rome in '80. The book takes up where '77 Sulphate Strip left off and continues for the next 20 years during which I became a pop magazine publisher and launched several titles including Flexipop (that featured an exclusive flexi disc on the cover of each issue from bands like The Jam, The Pretenders, Adam & The Ants, Genesis, The Cure) and Pop Shop which ended up being owned by Robert Maxwell. Much of the book is made up of interviews in all four corners of the world with the likes of McCartney, Springsteen, Paul Weller, Sting, The Beach Boys, The Stones, John Denver, Barry White, The Sex Pistols, Blondie, The Clash, AC/DC, Earth Wind & Fire, Andy Williams, Don McLean, Bob Marley, The Who, you name it. I can't believe this dude was me.

What's your recollection of the whole Amsterdam hells angel experience at their clubhouse?

The scariest night of my life, apart from the time I saw a bloke get murdered in Manor House when I was 15. There's a pretty detailed account in Sulphate Strip.

What do you think they were like as people, The Stranglers? Do you think you saw a side to them where their guard was down that others didn't see?

Not sure if pop stars ever let down their guard. In the early days we'd sit in hotel rooms and get stoned and laugh and drink and laugh some more and everything was new and glistening and they clearly enjoyed the adulation. Who wouldn't? Besides, I don't think I was ever really comfortable around any star. I kept asking myself what right had I to be there which, I guess, made me some kind of schmuck. But I felt as relaxed with The Stranglers as I did with a band like Smokie who were sweet and low. They were four very different people. Hugh was high on life, Jean was high on devotion, Dave was high on mystery and Jet was high on years. And they blended like a strawberry and banana smoothie.

What was the best Stranglers gig you ever saw?

It's like asking 'what's your all time favourite song'. It's impossible to answer. Every time they took to the stage you didn't know what would happen – with them or the crowd. In Iceland the audience punched the shit out of each other, in Amsterdam the Angels punched the shit out of the audience, in Brighton the audience spat like snakes, in Rome they threw cans, in Battersea the strippers came out to play, in Tokyo the band incited a riot as they did in Nice. They didn't take prisoners and you didn't want them to. It's what made them special.

Do you think the whole sexism thing they were labelled with was true or unfair?

I think a majority of bands back then were kinda sexist, only they didn't realise it. When sex is on tap, cynicism can grow hard and erect. A lot of pop music was sexist thirty years ago. It was NME that first pointed the finger and the band found it all faintly amusing. Very few journalists liked the band as people, though they grudgingly admired their music, and they were always looking for ways to slap them down. It certainly didn't affect Stranglers' record sales, that's for sure.

Do you think they were one of, if not *the* best group of their era?

For sheer excitement, they were up there with The Pistols, Clash, Damned, Jam and Johnny Thunders. For sheer showmanship they were up there with The Pistols, Clash, Damned, Jam and Johnny Thunders. For sheer passion they were up there with The Pistols, Clash, Damned, Jam and Johnny Thunders. But for sheer musicianship, The Stranglers were the best of the punk pack and that's what set them apart. It was all about Dave's organ, and shit, did he have a big one.

RATTUS NORVEGICUS

In the mid 70s, the live album was beginning to look like it could remould the key to a successful rock album. Dr Feelgood, those proto punk pub rockers, had got to Number One in the UK with their brilliant album Stupidity, which was recorded live on tour in 1975. UA were keen to capture The Stranglers live sound for record, due to the band's brilliantly raw feel. One thing the fans loved about The Stranglers music was the strange, heavy bass sound of JJ Burnel; it was unlike any other sound out there. Hugh attributed the distinct sound to accidental chance rather than precise detail. Hugh: "Jean had a speaker cabinet about the size of a door with 16 or so 10" speakers which are a bit too small to be taking bass. They all blew one after the other so he ended up with a huge bass cabinet with blown speakers but the sound got dirtier and dirtier and became a feature of the band."

In my opinion JJ is among the top bass players in the history of rock music. Technically he has created some of the most complex and strange bass licks (check out the end of Straighten Out for example), while the way he plays it, as if he were taking out all his troubles with raging, hard thuds of his fists, is totally out of this world. Never had a bass player sounded so angry, so loud and so brilliant. He was definitely the only great bass player of the era and JJ, looking back, sees this too.

"Well, none of them were as good as me, that's for sure! But some of them did great stuff. Peter Hook did some great stuff; I mean, how can a guy play with his bass on the floor? That amazes me. Captain

Sensible was a pretty good bass player. Jah Wobble was alright; nice style, I'll give him that, and Foxton was fine except he always made me wanna go, 'Look at the audience, you cunt!' Some people hide behind their instrument, looking at the fret board all the time. Some just look at their shoes, or hide behind their hair... Loads of good bass players, but none of them could approach me in speed (listen to Mr Modesty), or had the variety, lyricism and melody [laughs.] So there."

UA had to capture the key elements of the band for their LP. It was a well observed fact that the band needed little tweaking in the studio, hence their initial decision to make their debut LP a live one. Jim Evans wrote of one Stranglers London show at The Nashville, "The show was being recorded for a live LP, which must have chart potential. They're big in London now and could be big right across the land if their record gets good airplay. Presentation: Seven out of ten. Why does the organist look so bored? Content: Nine out of ten. Their songs are strong, especially Peaches. Entertainment value: ten out of ten!"

The live LP, to be titled Dead on Arrival, proved to be not such a good idea after all. Whenever the band tried to record a gig for the album it never came out quite right. Plus the title Dead on Arrival was not only negative and pretty lame, it was just inviting clever little critical put downs and puns from the music press. It was then decided they should record it in a proper recording studio after all, that way attention could be paid to getting it just right. Plus the possibility of making tiny tweaks to their sound was at least an option.. So well rehearsed the band were (due to all that constant gigging) Rattus Norvegicus, now the decided title, was recorded very quickly indeed. The tracks were well honed and the band were tight and well oiled. It took only six days to record the lot. "We could play those songs in our sleep," said Jet. "There are a lot of nerves on those early albums, but somehow it all hanged together, you know."

Although Rushent is lauded as a great producer, Hugh stated he did little of the work on the Rattus sessions, claiming TW Studio's engineer Alan Winstanely did all the work and Rushent "got the beers in and told jokes." Listening to the album, I think Martin has a real ear for thorough and unmistakable melody and a knack for fine mixing. He brought The Stranglers to life on this record!

33 years on, Rattus sounds unbelievably fresh, vibrant, urgent, tough and pulsating with aggression. From its opening number, the hard rocking Sometimes, to its sweeping 8 minute closer, Down in the Sewer, it is an unforgettable album full of amazingly catchy songs with an atmosphere that the band never again quite captured. The first track, Sometimes opens with a heavy beat, a rough punk drive powered by one of Burnel's most vicious, thumping bass lines and Hugh's imprecise, scratchy chords, over which Dave Greenfield's gothic organ adds an air of mystery and strangely, the sad regret of uncontrollable violence. The lyrics in it are the typical kind that got the band labelled as misogynists in the first place. From the opening lyric about smacking a girlfriend's face, one might instantly think these guys are a bunch of sweaty, oafish, women hating thugs. But listen on and you may work it out. In truth, the song is based on what Hugh calls "an unpleasant experience" involving a situation where he slapped his girlfriend after finding out she had been cheating on him with another man. The feeling of anger from Hugh is one mixed with hurt and upset, not a sense of satisfaction from the pointless, macho overpowering of a female. From the first line in their first

ever recorded song, the Stranglers sound sexist, and it seems they delight in bullying and pushing women around for no reason. Here begins case two in the canon of classic Stranglers mislabelling.

For years the band found it impossible to shake off these sexist accusations. As far on as 1981 the boys were still defending the controversial lyrics on Rattus to ever angry female journalists. In the NME, January 1981, Lynn Hanna had made her mind up about The Stranglers before she had even met them. She writes;

"I tell Hugh Cornwell that a lot of women, including myself, found the lyrics on the first two Stranglers albums threatening and offensive. Cornwell, adopting a lofty air of detachment replies blandly, 'I'm surprised you found them threatening. Maybe that demonstrates your own insecurity'." She asks Hugh "But women aren't secure from violence are they?" Hugh says "That shows that a lot of women are insecure." "Yes," she replies, "But you were playing on those insecurities." "Not at all," says Cornwell, "I was playing on my guitar." Hanna goes on to ask Hugh about the lyrics in Sometimes, in particular the line that reads, "Beat you till you drop." Hugh defends his art in the intense interrogation. "That was a particular situation where the girl is unfaithful and the guy reacts violently. It happens all the time. It's just a document of life."

To fully understand the sexist claims launched at The Stranglers, you must take a proper look at the cultural scope of Britain at that time. The 1970s were simply the most carelessly sexist of times, where nudity was thrown about without the slightest bat of an eye lid. Good old days. It wasn't considered a bad thing to look at women as sex objects and it still isn't; even now, bare breasts remain a big part of British culture, most notably on page 3 of our most popular newspaper every single day. If that isn't "sexist" I don't know what is. Most rock bands in the 70s were misogynistic, at least if you line them up to the same standards that got The Stranglers branded as pigs. Take a look at the album covers of Roxy Music, Whitesnake or The Scorpions. Rock and roll goes hand in hand with this sort of dehumanised sexual infatuation. It must also be noted that punk, and the beliefs of punk, held very little importance over sex, or as Johnny Rotten called it "squelching." Perhaps the Stranglers' leery, women loving ways stood out more in that oh so sexless and politically aimed movement. The Stranglers defence to me is in their music's obvious aspect of social commentary. They were the artist reflecting the emotion; in this case the emotion was sexual depravity and lust.

Phil McNeil however noted that Rattus could bring females to tears of humiliation; a nice case of exaggeration there I am sure.

In 1977, after Rattus had been released and was basically storming the charts, one can look back at the reckless behaviour and words of the band as slightly exaggerated and one can clearly see the blatantly tongue in cheek comments for what they are; an inspired effort to ruffle a few feathers. "Well I ended up hitting my girlfriend," Hugh told Melody Maker, "and I felt very powerful afterwards. We're not criticising women, we are just observing behaviour. And sure we have a vested interest in not changing. Men do think of women as sex objects. That's just an observation."

Which brings us to Peaches. After Grip, the band's musically upbeat study of the hardest times of life in a rock group stalled at Number 44 (after a chart mix up), Peaches was released as the follow up single. The band were selling out gigs all over the UK now and the disappointment of Grip was very much seen as a total mix up, hence UA's decision to quickly make an album and release the now legendary, Peaches as a 45. A mutated, perverted reggae track, Peaches was an instant hit, reaching number 8 on the UK charts and staying in the top 40 for 14 weeks, two years after it had originally been written. The B side, Go Buddy Go went back even further than The Stranglers early days; JJ had written it in the 1960s as a teenager, clearly influenced by the early rock n roll songs of Chuck Berry. On the back of this success, the band appeared on Top of the Pops for the first time, lip synching very badly to the B side rather than the hit Peaches.

"The first time we were invited to appear on Top of the Pops," remembers Jet Black, "in keeping with our tradition of confusing, we were expected to trash the dressing room. It was widely reported that the BBC better watch out. When we got there we asked for some cleaning materials and a vacuum cleaner, and we completely cleaned the place up. People couldn't believe it and they still did not get the joke."

Back to Peaches; once again the sexist claims were slapped on the lads. The Stranglers were clearly not taking things too seriously and were basically expressing themselves as observers, commentators on social behaviour. Peaches, an ode to the fine art of leering at "chicks" is so tongue in cheek one finds it impossible to see why so many were offended by it. Admittedly the use of the words clitoris and shit were controversial (resulting in the cut radio edit) but the song is quite obviously harmless fun. Musically it has that unforgettable bass intro (recently voted the best intro of all time and the best bass line of all time in two polls) and comes into the irresistible, repetitive groove instantly. It is one of those songs that has entered the public's musical psyche and has stayed there firmly over the past 30 years. JJ and Hugh started writing the track after spending a night in a black club in Peckham where they had been enjoying some reggae. "We sat down and wrote peaches in the house when we got back." Hugh said. "Jean came up with the bass riff and I picked up and started playing around. Within ten minutes we had a bass run and a vocal." Peaches became a firm favourite in the band's live set, especially on the tour that backed the album, The Rats on the Road tour in May and June of 1977, but more of that later.

Peaches was slammed at the time for its apparent sexism, which was enhanced by such unforgettable music paper quotes as "We love women's movements, especially underneath us." Hugh defended the song. "Peaches was taken as an affirmation of the subject. I was making fun of it. But there you go, it shows how serious people were at the time. The Stranglers, although we were supposed to be serious hard nutters and the most punk, we were the ones with the sense of humour for god's sake." JJ also defended with, "It was as if we invented sexism, or we were the first sexist rock group in the world. Bloody joke, you know."

Listeners also picked up on the misogyny with tracks like London Lady and Princess of the Streets. Both songs are believed to be about JJs relationships, one casual, one close. London Lady is clearly about journalist Caroline Coon. On Coon's website, it clearly states, "In 1977 the New Musical Express stated that the Strangler's song 'London Lady' was written about Caroline Coon. In fact, the song is a woman-hating fantasy with lyrics indicative of what clinicians call 'small penis anxiety' and evidence of the sexism and misogyny that contaminates the male dominated music industry to this day."

Although the self obsessed Coon is referenced, the song also lingers over other areas such as the shallowness of groupies and women out to bed a star. "It's about empty headed women," said Hugh. "Women without personality. All they can talk about is what rock musician they laid the week before."

Burnel defended the lyrics to London Lady himself:

"We were drawing lots on who was going to screw this female column writer, and someone said, 'But it'd be like chucking a sausage up the Mersey Tunnel.' Someone else said, 'Dangling a piece of string in a bucket' - it's been done before, so we decided it wasn't valid to do it. It's just about some chicks in a very small scene. It's not a 'retrogressively sexist song',"

Princess of the Streets is totally an ode to The Doors. With JJ on lead vocals, he admitted it was his opportunity to do a Jim Morrison impression. It is by far better than London Lady which is the most typical of 77 punk and is perhaps the weakest track on the album. But that is no put down, as this is one good album indeed

Musically and lyrically, we had subjects as odd as the predictions of Nostradamus on Goodbye Toulouse; a frantic rocker which explains the haunting predictions of the French seer who claimed one day that Toulouse would be destroyed in a nuclear explosion. On Hanging Around, the band gave us a sweaty, even more acid soaked Doors trip down London's sleazy haunts and gay bars, like the Colherne. Musically it is hypnotic and one gets lost in the amazing interplay between Hugh's wiry guitar licks and Dave's multi layered keys. Burnel's bass growls like a warning of trouble looming in the city streets and Jet pounds away on the drums like the engine that powers the whole group; the tune is perfect and it also features one of

Cornwell's most excellent guitar solos. Why this wasn't a single I don't know, as it is possibly the single greatest moment in the Stranglers whole back catalogue.

Ugly, a powerful, aggressive JJ penned track is perhaps the most out right controversial track on the album. JJ shouts about beauty not being in the eye of the beholder, the sickening appearance of acne, coffee laced with sulphuric acid, two hideous freaks in a passionate moment, "an ugly fart" that attracts a good looking chick because of his wads of money, while also adding "it's different for Jews somehow." Hugh said of the track. "They're very subjective views. I hope in later life he would feel he was misguided." The words in Ugly are powerful, honest and very thought provoking. The fact that these strong words come across in the band's most out right aggressive and exciting rocker makes the album all the more fascinating. Ugly is the most experimental and free form song on the album and perhaps one of the reasons journalist Chas De Whalley famously renamed the band "Punk Floyd."

The most unpunk track has to be the album's closing track, the amazing, orchestral epic that is Down in the Sewer. In four parts, the Stranglers amaze us with this piece of urban sleaze, almost a symphonic sweep with a breath taking climax; the sewer being London and the rats the people in it, full of disease. With tracks like this the band proved they had so much more to offer than all the other punk groups put together. It is musically astounding, especially Greenfield's spiralling organ solo and Hugh's Hank Marvin esque guitar riff.

In the press, every shocking accusation was thrown at the Stranglers. Melody maker noted "the fierce examples of chauvinism," and gave the album a less than flattering review. The NME's Phil McNeil gave it a notoriously critical review, drawing relentlessly on the "oafish" manner of the group and commenting that Peaches "was demeaning just listening to it". While he also labelled it "drivel", even he couldn't deny that tracks like Grip, Hanging Around and Goodbye Toulouse were great.

But looking back, the album's sound is truly amazing. One of the best and most straight forward record producers, Martin Rushent did an excellent job recording the songs. "Because of the way they were done it was actually quite relaxed." Martin said. "We used the same sounds throughout and let the band make alterations for each song as they did live, so we'd get the sound at the beginning of the album and then it was just a matter of checking each day to make sure no mics had moved. We'd do one run-through to check levels, then three performances back to back, before moving on. We may have edited some takes together but the object was to pick the best one. Then we'd slam on the vocals and instrument overdubs. We already had the mics, compressors and the Harmonizer all set up, so it wasn't exactly hard work. We bashed the vocals out in no time and they sounded great. I loved making those records."

The wall of guitars (an overdub suggested by Rushent) and the grumbling bass on Grip give the song so much vibrant energy. It was all there ready to be put down on vinyl. Other than the odd sound effect (nuclear explosion on Toulouse, rats and sewage on the end of Down in the Sewer) the record contains very few ruffles; the band's collective sound created and oozed a certain atmosphere on its own anyway.

The full title of the album was actually Rattus Norvegicus: IV, a deliberate attempt at confusing the public. On a visual level one cannot ignore the striking image on the album cover. Rather than opting for the original concept, a rat scurrying across a bright orange sunset beneath the Stranglers iconic logo, the band were shot in makeup, standing menacingly in a dimly lit mansion in Blackheath; the place they filmed many of the Hammer studio horror films. It is an eerie, unforgettable image and a perfect fit for the seedy contents within the sleeve.

Staying in the charts for the whole year, it is astonishing to think that they achieved this fame with next to no airplay. John Peel regularly played the band but also noted that none of his colleagues were putting them on the airwaves. Good old Peel.

Jet explains, "The singles didn't get much airplay on the radio. The BBC hated us, they never played us on Radio 1, very rarely anyway, so they didn't get exposure and people didn't know about the singles, whereas they knew for some reason about the albums and bought them."

INTERVIEW WITH
MARTIN RUSHENT

What was your previous experience prior to Rattus and how did The Stranglers management decide on using you?

Well I had been a studio engineer for many years at a studio called Advision and I had worked with lots and lots of different people, one of them people being Shirley Bassey. And Shirley Bassey's producer was a chap called Martin Davies who at the time ran UA records. Shirley was signed to that label. The head of A and R there was a chap called Andrew Lauder, who was one of the greatest A and R men ever. But Martin Davies thought he had a problem because he didn't understand studios. He knew a good band when he heard it but he didn't know how to get the good record out of the band. So Martin Davies offered me a job as Andrew's assistant, with special responsibility for getting the bands recorded. So on my first day there he played me a demo of Get a Grip on Yourself by The Stranglers. He said 'I am thinking of signing this band, what do you think?' So I said, 'Well on the strength of that song I would sign them tomorrow'. We went to see them at the Red Cow in Hammersmith. So I said 'I'll do it, I'll produce them for you'. And he said, 'Look we don't want it overproduced, we just want it slammed in there to capture the energy of the band.' I said 'I couldn't agree with you more' and we went and did Grip first, that sort of charted not very high up, but it showed us we were on the right track. So we all agreed and went back in to record as many as we could. And in the space of 10 days we knocked out all Rattus and half of No More Heroes.

Not bad going really is it?

Not bad at all. I wish it was this quick these days.

Exactly. What did you think of The Stranglers, as people when you first met them?

Um.... Now, I am considering that question. Obviously they were all different characters. I felt that to an extent that they were acting up a bit. They wanted to project this image of being tough and aggressive which was part of their show, but they did it all the time, instead of saving it for the stage. So I felt underneath it all they were just four ordinary blokes that put on this veneer of being really hard and punky, but actually weren't wholly that at all. You know, so I just used to ignore it all.

Was there a lot of tension in the studio when they were recording?

No, not really. I think it's fairly common knowledge that Jean Jacques and me didn't really get on that well. We worked quite successfully together but our relationship deteriorated over time. But I got on brilliantly with all of them at the time of the Rattus sessions. We had a real laugh doing it really.

This is when they were more naive; did fame change this?

Well yeah I suppose so. I have probably changed too. Success does change people even if you don't think it does. It also changes people's attitudes towards you, which is a tricky one to deal with. In my career, the attitude of my whole family changed towards me. I could detect the changes so, yeah, obviously success does have an effect on you, whether it's a negative or a positive one it depends on the individual in question.

Do you have any fond memories or stories of Rattus that perhaps nobody knows about?

(Laughs) That nobody know about? I think the funniest thing of all was, the last track we were doing at TW Studios, which was a really small studio on Fulham Palace road and the studio used to go out under the streets. You couldn't hear the cars above, but we knew we were out in the streets. The control room was under a launderette. So it was the last night of the sessions and the last thing we did was Down in the Sewer for Rattus. It must have been no more than about half an hour after we left, that the rear wall of the studio collapsed and Fulham palace sewer emptied its contents into the studio. Which I think is really odd.

Very fitting to the song.

Yeah absolutely. That was something I will never forget. I just imagine, because it was right at the place where Jet used to sit and play his drums. I just imagined it happening when we were recording Down in the Sewer, and Jet getting covered in shit would have been really funny. But unfortunately that didn't happen.

Were you surprised by the success of Rattus?

(Long pause). Yes, I was surprised by the scale of the success. I thought it would take a while for sales to build as more people got to hear the record. But what we didn't realise was that the band had been gigging all over the country for ages, and had done hundreds of dates and had built up a really big following out there that wasn't obvious. So when we put the album out there they all bought it in the first week, it just went straight in at number 4 and we were all like "WHAT?" So I always believed it was a great album and always believed it would be a success but the speed of its success caught me by surprise; it caught us all by surprise I think.

Do you still rate it highly now, the content of it?

Oh yeah! I think Rattus Norvegicus and No More Heroes are the two supreme Stranglers albums, after that I think it was a bit of a downhill run. Whilst there are certain tunes on Black and White that I like, as an album I don't think it stands up to those first two. There isn't a dud on Rattus and there isn't a dud on No More Heroes, but on Black and White I think we were losing the plot. It was after Black and White that I said 'I'm not doing it anymore, I think you've gone off the boil and probably need fresh ears."

Was it definite that you'd be returning to produce their second album?

From my point of view I don't think there was any discussion about it. There may have been on The Stranglers side, but I wouldn't have been a part of that and wouldn't know. But the general consensus was that I had just produced an album that had broke them through; United Artists wanted me to do it, the management wanted me to do it, half of it was already recorded from the Rattus sessions so that's what ended up happening. Whether the band wanted to try someone else I wouldn't know, you'd have to ask them.

Had the atmosphere in the studio changed from the first album?

No. It was still very much the same vibe. I can't recall any particular problems. Jean and Hugh were still getting on; I mean there were rows; there always is when you're making a record. It was very much a repeat of Rattus.

What did you set out to achieve sound wise for this album?

I think it was clear to me that what I think the public wanted was more of the same. I think it was too early for the Stranglers to strike out in a new direction. If we brought out an album that had been radically different from Rattus I think everyone would have been disappointed.

Any great memories?

I know we had a lot of laughs. I used to bore them with the plans of my new swimming pool which everyone took the piss out of. They used to say 'ooh you're moving out to the country, big fucking rock star thing.' The thing was I had been living in the country for years before I had even met them, I was just moving house. Rattus and Heroes were great fun to do.

What did you think to the new songs from Black and White when you first heard them?

I liked some of them and some of them I had problems with. I liked Toiler on the Sea and Nice n Sleazy. There were others like Tank that I found difficult. Sweden was alright but it didn't set me alight. I thought what had happened was, to be fair to the band, all songs on Rattus and Heroes had been written before they had a record contract, before they were famous, in capital letters, and while they had the time to write. Not only that, those songs had been worked up and taken out in front of an audience. So when we got them in the studio it was perfect. Black and White was the first time they had to write with all the pressures of touring and fame. Also they hadn't been played out live much before they had been recorded. I think they were also trying to move on a bit, which is a good idea on the third album. It was hell making it. It wasn't any fun for me. Jean and Hugh were starting to fall out. Where before I would do a mix and they might have a few minor criticisms and they were happy if I went back and polished it, the mixing of Black and White just seemed to go on forever. I mean I was flying back and forward to New York, because that's where they were. It became a little too much. So when it came to the fourth album, I had done Live X Cert, which I don't like. I don't think I captured them properly. They had done five nights at The Roundhouse. There were terrible rows between Hugh and JJ. I don't know what they were over. There was obviously some fracturing appearing in their relationship, which was obviously gave me cause for concern. When it came to the Raven album I thought I had gone as far as I could with them. For their sake they needed a new mentor. Because I admit I love the first two albums so much I could have gone on making that style of music for the rest of my life and been very happy with it.

Yeah, you have to look at it from your point of view too. You're a producer; you have to keep making stuff you have in faith in.

Well yeah. I became a record producer because I didn't want to work in a bank or digging roads. I wanted to do something that was fun and challenging. If working with an artist becomes anything other than that I don't want to do it.

You have had an amazing career; you could go on all day about the stuff you have done.

I have been very fortunate. I always do stuff I enjoy doing, so the moment it becomes like work you're in trouble. And it was during Black and White that I felt as if I was going to work.

Was much of the fun lost in the outrageous behaviour in the band? Were they acting out of control?

(Sighs) Yeah, but not all of them. Jean certainly was. His attitude towards women, I am still trying to figure out if it was a pose because they were getting slammed for being sexist and chauvinist. Some of his antics were totally outrageous; whether he was playing up to that label for effect or whether he was a genuine misogynist, I don't know.

It's like you said before when we were on Rattus, they seemed to be pretending to be people they weren't, but never actually stopped acting that way.

That's right, yeah. It just didn't feel right for me to go on. They needed someone new. It wasn't fair for them and it wasn't fair for me.

I have read that friction was caused with you by some of JJ's antics. Wasn't there an incident with your receptionist?

That was my secretary. He went up to United Artists and I think he tried to rip her bra off from what I understand. She phoned me from the studio and she was very upset. I mean you can't be doing that, it's just not on. So yeah we fell out big time over that. I just didn't like the man he was becoming. But I want to be fair to everybody; we were all kids who had this amazing success and I don't think any of us handled it well. Some of the things I was doing were not exactly the thing I would do now as a mature individual. But if suddenly you're making loads of money and everyone wants to talk to you and you're flavour of the month it is tough to handle. It happens so quickly.

We look back now and see JJ and Hugh at the forefront of the band but what were Jet and Dave like?

Oh brilliant! Jet was the sort of guy who could play... well firstly he was a lovely bloke, really nice, great sense of humour, really friendly. You couldn't wish to meet a nicer guy. Then he just sat there and played rock solid drums all fucking day long; totally reliable. I can't recall a time when Jet made a single clanger. Really reliable, rock solid drummer. Nothing is too much trouble for him. Dave was a bit of a genius I think. He was sort of, well, to describe him as an odd guy wouldn't be correct, but he was into black magic and white witch craft and that stuff as a hobby. I have seen him playing these left handed complex pieces on his Hohner pianette or whatever it was, and thrashing out complex chords on his Hammond organ. Then in the middle of it all, he'd grab his can of special brew and drink half of it, put it back down and carry on. Then if he didn't have any organ work he would do all that wiggly stuff on his pianette......drinking special brew. Extraordinary man and quite a deep person as well; a deep thinker.

Did you go on the infamous Iceland trip?

I did. I didn't see much of the band there. What happened was UA decided to reward all their staff, who had worked really hard in promoting The Stranglers and making a success of it. So UA management decided to reward the whole firm. 'Right, we're all going to Iceland for three days to see The Stranglers.' So we all piled on this plane, all the band and everybody flew over and we all got hepatitis from something we ate. Not the serious one, the one that lays you low for a few weeks. So everyone was off sick, the office was virtually closed. That was Iceland's gift to us. Other than that, it was in June so we'd all go to a club and come out at three a.m. to see the sun blazing down. Very odd. I don't remember anything crazy going on in that trip.

Didn't Grant and Davies want to resign around this time?

While I did speak to the management, over logistical issues or the progress of the album, it didn't have much to do with the relationship between The Stranglers and the management. I was made aware from general social chit chat that they weren't too happy. I never knew what went on there; I really don't know. There are several artists from around that time, Hazel O Connor being one, who I still work with from time to time, who are not happy about that period,

But more than that I can't say because I was never a part of what went on. Did anyone rip anyone off? I have no idea.

So you were just involved in the musical side really weren't you?

That's right. I wasn't a party of meetings or agreements between the artists and the management.

Probably the best way really isn't it?

I think so yeah. In retrospect I was just wide eyed and innocent. All I wanted to do was make hit records. The business end of it wasn't something I ever thought about. I knew I would get paid so it wasn't a problem to me. Whereas for The Stranglers of course, they had to deal with a lot of problems I didn't. Exactly what they were, I don't know.

Overall is the memory of working with The Stranglers good or bad?

Oh good! I had absolutely fantastic times with them. Once we had to do a radio promotional tour of America and the record company asked me to go with them. And we just had the funniest time; the things that happened were amazing, it was a riot all around. We got thrown out of radio stations. In Boston the police had to come and sort of.... Jean had just done this interview with the Melody Maker where he said that Americans had smaller brains than Europeans. That didn't make us too popular with the red necks. And when that news broke in America we were in a Boston radio station doing interviews and suddenly they were calling in saying 'What the fuck is all this about? You limey bastards!' And if my memory serves me correctly we had to be escorted out of the building by the police because a nasty crowd had gathered outside in the street. It was just one thing after another mate. So it was insanity all the way round; we lost Hugh in Detroit, he had gone to some party and we didn't have a fucking idea where he'd gone. An absolute riot.

I know The Stranglers aren't normally really categorized as a punk band but do you think they were punk in their attitude and how they were?

It's a difficult one this. I mean I never considered The Stranglers as a punk band, I think they stand apart if you compare them to the Pistols, The Clash or The Damned. They were much more skilled than the others. They were a rock band with a punk edge. But because they came up in that punk era, they had to play the game. But I don't think they were a punk band. Aggressive, powerful, demanding of attention, fucking loud; they were all of those things. But they were that anyway. But they were a rock n roll band with a unique edge but they got bundled in with that whole punk thing because that was what was going on at the time. You understand what I mean?

Definitely!

They are one of my favourite bands. The original Stranglers line up, Rattus Norvegicus and No More Heroes period; my favourite band of

all time. I feel really privileged to have worked with them. Wait I've got someone at my front door, hold on a second.
(I hear Martin opening the door and what appears to be the sound of vicious hounds barking).
Come in Sammy, I'm just doing a quick interview.

Do you think they were one of the great bands?

Oh yeah. I think history has been very good to them. I think they are highly respected now and if they weren't respected as much as they should have been in their day, who fucking cares, frankly? Now, their work from this period is highly respected. It is tough to turn on the telly nowadays without hearing a Stranglers song from that era.

The Keith Floyd documentary a few weeks back.

Exactly. It was all Rattus. It pops up in adverts and movies; it still sells. That has to be, what is it now, 35 years ago? If a piece of music can still be popular and still be played 30 odd years later, then that is a testament isn't it?

It's what really matters isn't it?

Yes. Who else can you look at? The Clash are still played today. The Pistols, yes, although I'm not a big fan of the Pistols. It's all a racket now, that.

Buzzcocks!

Yeah, Buzzcocks; another one of mine. Bands like The Lurkers and Generation X you can see them as second division now. And The Damned,

NO MORE HEROES

"There's gonna be a gig, with The Grateful Dead, The Beach Boys and Yes, all using the same equipment and it's gonna be in the archaeology department at the Ritz museum."
- Hugh Cornwell, Amsterdam Paradiso September 1977

"We were in the top 10 the whole of 1977. We were selling more than everyone that year so the punters really liked us but the media was anti Stranglers. During the Heroes tour Tony Parsons went on the road with us and wrote it up that we were Nazi homosexual thugs. The Pistols were everywhere from 1976. The tabloids were revelling in the so called naughtiness. We were cynical. We had a tabloid notoriety but we weren't mucking about. We were far more dangerous."

Although The Stranglers were now signed to UA and riding the wave of their new found success, the violence remained a frightening and overwhelming factor in the band's reputation. The aggression could no longer be blamed on the frustration at the lack of the band's success. Now it could perhaps be attributed to JJ settling in and relishing in his new hard man reputation, the band keeping up to their expected public persona and as a reaction against some of the more confrontational members of the crowd. Hugh amusingly sums it up with, "Jean used to launch himself into the audience a lot. He used to love flying through the air and landing on people's heads."

The Stranglers were by now publicly known as shocking, violent, scary thugs; sexist and frightening to the journalists who took every opportunity to bad mouth them. Their publicity was very thoroughly thought out and perhaps wrongly, Alan Edwards enhanced the fact the Stranglers attracted and dished out violence frequently by occasionally embellishing their antics. For the moment it was all harmless fun, any publicity being good publicity. But in the long run, this damaged the progression of the band, their amount of radio air play and their general reputation. But in 1977, The Stranglers were massive and somehow they have managed to soldier on for over 30 years, despite all the odds being against them.

The Rats on the Road tour tore through the country, attracting controversy and outrage wherever it went. Many gigs were cancelled due to the councils slapping a ban on The Stranglers, who many felt were "undesirable." Comments like "We don't want this kind of thing in our town!" spread across the newspapers and press, like terrified warnings of a plague of disease. Speaking in 2009, JJ Burnel spoke of the violence of the late 70s that was so big a part of The Stranglers reign of the UK charts and how he has managed to overcome it in his later years.

"I've beaten up a few people. I teach karate so I've sorted out that side of myself, but when I was younger I was very thin-skinned. I wanted to fit in and be English, but wasn't allowed to be, so became an aggressive, violent little sod with a chip on my shoulder. I now understand how immigrant kids feel. They want to be part of this culture but are bullied, racially abused and not accepted. I discovered karate was a path to enlightenment and peace. My karate master in Japan, Kancho Soeno, is very gentle and the font of much wisdom.

The Japanese are into Zen and Shinto, nature and ancestors, and the idea that things improve with age. In the West our bodies degenerate and we get narrow-minded and materialistic, yet we should be going the opposite way, getting fitter and stronger and less dependent on material wealth."

Fights on the tour were frighteningly violent. After a gig in Canterbury, fifty thugs waited outside the venue for the band. The heaviest hard nuts really were attracted to the violent appeal of punk rock, if not for the musical aspect then perhaps for the chance to challenge one of these so called tough guy punk rock leaders to a fight. With The Stranglers though, they certainly met their match. JJ went outside accompanied by Dennis Marks and confronted the thugs, running at them with a mike stand. By the time the other Finchley Boys got outside, the scrap was dying out, although one Finchley Boy did recall saving JJ from literally being stabbed in the back.

At a gig in Winter Gardens, June 77, a group of Grimsby Dockers came along to cause some trouble. Not only did they heckle the support bands relentlessly, they even beat up two teenage girls in the crowd. This really pissed JJ off and he challenged all of them to a fight. As Burnel put down his bass, a bear of a man suddenly climbed on to the stage and approached him. Burnel rose to the challenge of the Incredible Bulk before him and proceeded to kick the shit out of the said beast, before tripping him over on to his back with a sweep kick. What followed can best be described as a bloodbath when the Dockers invaded the stage, resulting in a mass brawl where one thug was hospitalised after a cymbal slashed his face.

If this drama wasn't bad enough for the band, on the same night the restaurant staff in their hotel got snooty and wouldn't serve them a meal, saying that all the posh people were dining in there and The Stranglers didn't quite fit the bill. When the band flipped, the manager called the police. After much commotion the cops left, not before one officer was seen pushing Jet down a flight of stairs for no apparent reason.

Although their tour was going well on a commercial level, they still weren't reaping the benefits of their "sudden success". In a 1977 interview, JJ was asked if the money from Rattus was pouring in. JJ replied, "No, not really, we have to wait quite a while before the money comes through." And when he was asked whether the band make money on tour, he sharply said, "You're joking, it costs 60 quid a week for the van, 300 quid a week for the PA and 260 for the wages." In typically blunt, no nonsense form, JJ went on to express a lack of desire for conquering the states and being known as a musician. "We're going to America, but I'm not setting my sights on America, it's not a great ambition of any of us to woo America. It seems that British bands regard America as the be all and end all. It all depends on your motives. But I tell you, if it ever becomes like, "we'll play another tour for a new Rolls Royce" I hope I have the good sense to quit. I don't consider it to be work at the moment...to me work is a "four letter word." I don't see why any person should spend all their time doing something they don't really like doing. I guess that's the difference between a slave and an artisan. I don't regard myself as a musician, because musician implies work, a job, right? I mean, I know I can play rock n roll well, but I'm not a musician. I'd just like to have "rock n roller" on my passport."

On the money side of things, Cornwell recalls the unfair way in which the management handled the Stranglers funds. He said they would keep the band busy, constantly gigging, to keep their minds off the cash they had made. Then they would arrange tours, which were not only a financial loss, but were coming out of the band's wages as well. Of course the managers always got their cut no matter what. "I thought that was unfair practice, but it was the way people did it in those days."

Although The Stranglers were far from favourable towards the Americans, funnily enough their original press release after the unleashing of Rattus told another story. "The Stranglers will become big in America (a deal has been signed with A and M Records and Rattus Norvegicus is scheduled for release in late Summer). The Stranglers won't become just another big band. Already they are showing that they are capable of constant change and revision of their ideas and material."

It was when the band were becoming so often in the public eye that the outrage really began. The press slammed The Stranglers at every and any opportunity. "All over the world," JJ said, "the press weren't very nice. It's probably because we weren't very nice. But also there was a kind of political situation between the Stranglers and the rest of the bands. The Pistols, The Clash and the press were on one side and we were on the other, so for years we had no support. But we still sold more records than them."

JJ doesn't regret his aggressive behaviour of the late 70s, but looks back on it realistically. "It was fun at the time," he has since said. There are countless stories involving JJ dishing out the beatings and some have entered an almost mythical status within the fans minds and of those of the rock press. Journalists would shudder and shake at the thought of interviewing The Stranglers. And why? Well, you may already know the many tales that make The Stranglers such bad boys, but if you don't, you will soon find out.

The Stranglers, apparently, kept an empty jug on stage and if the frequent spitting of a particular punter got on their nerves, they would piss in it and throw it all over the front row. Then they would say, "Now you're all Stranglers piss heads!" Hugh was recently asked how the band dealt with hecklers and those keen on gobbing at them. He replied, "Our bass player used to get off stage and beat the shit out of them. Then we'd wait for him. 'You finished yet?' Then we'd carry on with the number." In truth there must be hundreds of middle aged men out there who can say they got chinned by JJ Burnel; and you never know, some of them might even be proud of it. Of course, an old banana up the arse was occasionally used to teach hecklers a lesson, but this is a little harder to justify.

"It could be quite harrowing," Hugh said of the intimidation of these gigs. "In fact a gig that passed without any incident was a rare event. The music was so belligerent and the audiences were intimidated. Like a lot of people when they are intimidated, they reacted physically. So there were constant incidents."

Listening to live recordings from this era shows the band on truly shocking punk form. One show in particular, recorded in February in Middlesbrough has an impatient crowd heckling relentlessly while Hugh changes a string. "What's the matter cunt?" says Jet calmly, "You never seen a broken string before?" The Stranglers were punk - no doubt about it.

"We're already bringing changes," said Hugh Cornwell, "In Something Better Change we are just saying we want to see more action, sociological changes, structural changes and we want to see it happen more quickly. We feel we have a responsibility and an obligation. People are looking at the crest of the new wave for change, breaking new ground. Innovation and all that."

In June of 1977, UA pressed The Stranglers to get back into the studio to record a follow up album. The label could see that punk would fizzle out and wanted to get as much cash out of this limited fad as possible. Seeing as Rushent and the band had recorded enough tracks for half a new album left over from the Rattus sessions, they only had to get a few more new numbers written and recorded for the follow up. Peasant in the Big Shitty, a surreal nightmare about a bad acid trap, the epic rocker School Mam, the catchy hit to be Something Better Change and the old favourite Bitching had already been put down. Dagenham Dave, the ode to their legendary, late admirer was recorded and given a high energy production, while songs like Burning up Time (a song that name checked the Finchley Boys as well as capturing the excitement of the band's storming success) and English Towns were written to order, the latter considered an album filler. The most controversial songs on the album were I Feel Like a Wog, which sounds like exactly what it isn't and Bring on the Nubiles, quite simply the most ridiculously offensive song they ever wrote. I Feel Like a Wog is basically a tale of urban alienation, where Hugh and the band sympathise with outsiders and immigrants, while saying you don't have to be from another country to feel victimised by society. The music springs constantly and causes one to move; the bass line is strong,

Greenfield's organ swirls and Black's thudding beat is relentless. Hugh shouts the lyrics with real anger; this is his country and even he feels out of place in it. The Stranglers were definitely not racist one bit, but they knew putting that word in a song title would be controversial. Jet insisted the band were far from prejudiced.

"I take people as I find them; I don't find race is a problem. I mean, a black man, a Jew or an Arab; if he's a nice person to be with, it's great! I'm not interested what colour he is or what church he goes to. I judge him for what he is."

Bring on the Nubiles was basically a big wind up, deliberately written to shock and outrage the press even further. Already branded sickening, thuggish, sexist pigs, Nubiles, although so obviously a joke gone too far, enraged their critics even more. With a lyric like "let me let me fuck ya fuck ya," it was clear the motive of the song was an experiment in seeing just how far they could push it. "Every song we write is in praise of women," Hugh said, "yet everyone thinks we hate them."

The original sleeve cover, a picture of JJ lying on a replica of Trotsky's grave was rejected by the band, in the end replaced by a rose covered wreath, mourning the dead heroes of yesteryear. The album was to be called No More Heroes.

Something Better Change, the follow up single to Peaches, sounds like a real effort on the band's part to create a memorable punk anthem. The riff is simple, addictive and hummable; it reached Number 8 on the UK charts. Upon its release Melody Maker noted, "The follow up to Peaches. A double A side (with Straighten Out) by the band generally regarded as the most musically interesting of the new wave leaders."

The title track of the album had begun to take shape shortly after the release of Rattus. Now, the song sticks out not only from the Stranglers musical output but from the general pop charts of the time. Released as a single, it reached Number 8, following in the steps of Something Better Change, becoming an anthem of the punk era. All these years on it is still as fresh as it was back then; a classic of the genre and one of the key musical moments of its era. The riff, like Peaches and most of the band's best material, started off as a JJ bass riff that Hugh and the rest of the band then worked on to perfection. The keyboard work on No More Heroes is particularly brilliant.

The lyrics, penned by Cornwell, are very memorable. Hugh remembered the inspiration behind them;

"The week before we wrote it Groucho Marx and Elvis had died in the same week. They had always been there in my life and suddenly they weren't there anymore." Bootlegs of the time hear Hugh screeching, "There's no more heroes so don't make anymore!" The Stranglers were lamenting the loss of real heroes in modern culture yes, but were also hinting at something else. "We even went through a period of not signing autographs," said Hugh. "We said 'what do you want our autograph for? Be your own hero.' We did that for a few years but couldn't keep it up." One night, JJ ended up attacking one fan that just wouldn't stop pestering him for an autograph. It seemed they were beginning to believe what the media was writing about them, and at times, taking it just a little too far. At the same time they were becoming heroes themselves.

Musically though, No More Heroes is for me the crowning glory in The Stranglers career; an amazing drive, unforgettable, catchy riff, a shiver inducing chorus and one of the best guitar solos in the history of popular music. It doesn't get any better than this!

As a complete album though, the press were not too impressed with Heroes, with many claiming it was too similar to Rattus in musical and lyrical content. Personally I disagree, thinking Heroes definitely sounds like the results of a band which is riding high and loving the glory of success, reeking of sleaze, fame and drug induced power. It is, in short, an acid punk classic. Scary psychedelia!

Some critics called the song writing shoddy, which is odd as half the tracks were left overs from the last album, an album which they supposedly all liked. "You could say there was a similar sound with the tracks on Rattus," admitted Hugh. The truth was they had to stick to a brand, for now at least, in a way to keep fresh in the minds of their public. What kind of a fool would you have to be to completely alter your sound a mere six months after your highly successful debut album? After all, change was to come later.

Harry Doherty in the Melody Maker wrote some interesting words about the record. "Very much the follow up to Rattus, not exactly going where no man has gone before but neatly stating musical and lyrical intentions. It doesn't have the same charm as the first album. I like it, I don't love it. Perhaps the answer lies in Something Better Change."

The critic Jon Savage famously disliked The Stranglers, never considering them big news and on the whole seeing them as pretty unspectacular. Famously he gave No More Heroes a 3 star review. Bastard! He branded the cover, a wreath with the No More Heroes text on it, as "hideous" and "chocolate box style." Some of the other words he used were "self indulgent," "I think it sucks," "embarrassing in parts," and bitterly adding "no doubt you'll all buy it anyway." JJ was insulted by Savage's review and one night tracked him down. He eventually found the critic drinking in a pub. Storming in accompanied by a Finchley Boy, JJ gave the bad mouthed critic a good old smack, calling him "an enemy of the revolution!" At the time, it may have seemed a good idea, but now, unfortunately, Savage has become the one key expert on the punk movement and is always a consultant whenever the word is brought up for TV shows or documentaries. His influential book on punk rock, England's Dreaming totally snubbed the Stranglers, despite them clearly being the most successful punk band of their day. Savage has made a living out of the punk movement and has used his own personal experience to rewrite history; very Stalinist.

After a recent documentary on punk was aired, one fan was shocked to see the exclusion, yet again, of the Stranglers.

"And once again, the Stranglers are left out of a punk retrospective. I wonder if this is because their message is just not PC enough for our modern sensibilities. OK, so they were a converted pub rock band from Guildford and Jet Black was/is about a hundred years old, but nonetheless they were at the forefront of the punk outrage in the UK. The first two albums are as dark and threatening as anything at the time. Anyone who says that the Stranglers were not one of the key 3 bands in punk in 1977.....just wasn't there."

In an American interview in 77, JJ said, "I've just hit one journalist because he's an enemy of the revolution and he's an idiot." He was clearly speaking about Jon Savage. Though behaviour like this was most certainly reckless, JJ was standing up for what he believed in. Plus, had the Stranglers not created so many shocking headlines in their prime, they would not be the great outsiders most fans remember them as today. You gotta love em! One reason I sympathise with the band is that the critics' put downs were often blatantly personal. Another side, as noted by Hugh, is that he would finish an interview thinking it had all gone smoothly, and that he and the reporter got on well. Then when he read the finished product he saw that the journalist had deceived him, pretended to agree on several areas in order to direct Hugh into comfortable, relaxed areas of free speech. Then the said reporter would paint a negative portrait of Cornwell, all of it based on deception. Deception is a big part in music journalism. "We feel like wogs all the time now," said Hugh.

"It used to bother us," said Jet, "It used to hurt our pride that we were misquoted and misused. But after a while we realised that it didn't make any bloody difference. What are we doing this for? We're doing this because we like doing it. So they can say what they like. It used to bug all the journalists that we were so honest and they couldn't handle it. We have met hundreds of journalists, but there are only a handful at the most that we have any kind of respect for. Most of them are just a bunch of arseholes. I mean they're real parasites."

Looking back on this era brews a special mix of fear and excitement within. These must have been scary times; constantly moving, incidents piling on top of each other rapidly. The Stranglers, in the midst of their success, may have been extremely controversial, but the bottom line is that their music was truly outstanding. Had this not been so, this outrageous behaviour would not be half as interesting; they would simply be just a bunch of obnoxious wind ups. But their songs were sharp, catchy and they had a sound like no other band. Even to this day no one has matched the pure filthy sound of vintage Stranglers. Combine this with an 'us versus the press' mentality and you have, as Jet Black called them, "the lepers of rock."

The band went on a second tour in 77 to support the album. When the No More Heroes tour expanded to Europe, Hugh once again found himself in Sweden, only this time the results were definitely not dull. The band was booked to play a gig in Kippen when a group of 200 members of a neo fascist party called the Ragarre invaded the concert. The group were apparently a cross between the Hells Angels and the National Front and in their masses they violently attacked the stage. The Stranglers managed to escape but the thugs caused a lot of damage to their gear and badly injured two roadies. The gang were strongly against punk rock, driving round in 1950s cars with greaser style haircuts listening to old rock n roll songs. They followed the band down the highway, howling for their blood and apparently brandishing chainsaws out of their car windows at them. This came near the end of the European leg of the tour, so the band cancelled their final two Swedish concerts and sharply exited the country, heading sharply back to Britain. Later, JJ shrugged off the laziness of gangs like the Ragarre, who steal from other cultures to form their own identities. "The Raggare think, 'Ahhh, American Graffiti, 50s, rock n roll', it's all laid out for them. Then you've got all the other wimps who think, 'ahh, Moscow or Perking'."

In one song on No More Heroes called Dead Ringer, musically a kind of sinister slant of Peaches, Greenfield howls cynically about people's need to follow trends, to join a gang or to belong to something just to achieve a sense of personal identity. Burnel was into Yukio Mishima, the famous author and poet who committed ritual suicide, quickly followed by his group of homosexual followers.

Burnel admired the group mentality and the honour of having control over your own death; the discipline of it all. Hugh never understood what he called "that male bonding thing." Differences in personalities were always a common factor within the group, only in 1977 the band were all pulling together in the same direction. They had to, given the amount of hostility coming at them from every corner of the globe.

The excitement of the No More Heroes tour continued. It was the biggest punk tour yet and the band became billboard superstars. Photographer Alan Perry recalled a gig in Coventry on the No More Heroes tour in October. "I remember that the smell of sweat during the mass pogo was horrendous!" They were now heavily into drugs and screwing any girl who happened to knock on the dressing room door. They were living the rock n roll lifestyle to the max, especially Hugh and JJ. Hugh has recalled that the band were having so much sex that they could barely remember who they had slept with a few days earlier. Although JJ had regular girlfriends from time to time, he didn't let this get in the way of bedding groupies at any and every opportunity. The Heroes tour had the band at the height of excess and the gigs were exciting, frantic spectacles of punk rock outrage.

Chris Brazier saw the band in Bournemouth: "The Stranglers were exhausted having spent the day wrangling with the old bill. I'm worried about some of their songs but not the performance of them. Lyrically many of them express a thoroughly nasty sexism through which women become nubiles, mere receptacles for men's lust. By all means revel in their music- a lot of it is great- but for heaven's sake think carefully about what they're saying."

In September 77, The Stranglers played two gigs at the grot hole that was The Amsterdam Paradiso, where the band were helped out on stage by the local chapter of Hell's Angels who acted as security for them. The Angels loved the Stranglers and it is easy to see why. The macho round up obviously saw much appeal in the hard man routine and reputation of these punk giants and when they arrived in Amsterdam, the Angels treated them like royalty.

"We were joined on stage by about 20 Hell's Angels," remembers Hugh, "I thought they were gonna kill me until one of them leant over to me and said, 'do you want these people off the stage?' because there were 2 or 3 people on the stage. So I said, 'as long as they stay out of the way and don't get in the way of the singing they can stay.' And he sort of went, 'OK.' And then afterwards they came downstairs into the dressing room and put a huge knife under my nose with about a gram of speed on it. I didn't want to be rude so I took the gram of speed. We became very good friends for a little while; it was a very funny experience."

They even invited the band back to their little club house, a scary place funded by the Government (I'm sure you can guess why) on the outskirts of Amsterdam. Journalist Barry Cain wrote about the experience;

"The clubhouse is tastefully lit, probably because most of the light bulbs have been smashed. Hugh plays pool with a guy affectionately referred to as Loser. His face has been eaten away by the acid shower he got in a bundle. A few fancy revs and in comes Jean Jacques on his Triumph bike along with an Angel on his Harley Davidson. Jean Jacques' mascara is smudged but he still retains his cucumber cool. Why the stunt? Bob Hart from The Sun is doing a feature on The

Stranglers/motorbikes/Hell's Angels and his photographer has set up a contrived but effective happy snap."

Publicist Alan Edwards was there that scary night, and he told me all about it:

"As the years progressed, the bigger the aggro, higher profile and tensions in the band became more acute. The days got stranger and stranger culminating in an alliance with the Hells Angels that started to see the group increasingly lose control. The vibe around the band got darker and they started to seem trapped in the environment that they had created. Fuelled by JJ's biker tendencies and The Stones like atmosphere around the group, The Stranglers were becoming hostages to fortune. A gig at the Paradiso in Amsterdam in the depths of winter highlighted just how dark the night was becoming. After the show we ended up at a Hells Angels club on the outskirts of the town. Outside a biker took pot shots at windows opposite from some sort of turret. Inside the atmosphere was decidedly heavy. Someone rode a Harley through the club and in a corner some Angels and their "old ladies" watched a home movie - some sort of gang bang! A bloke with a reconfigured face introduced himself to me at the bar and another gentleman put a gun to my temple. Time stood a bit still and everything took on a slightly filmic unreal air. I froze, as one does, probably the safest thing under the circumstances. They'd have sensed fear and if I'd panicked and ran for cover I might never have made it out in one piece. The trigger was pulled, everything happening in slow motion. No bang. Maybe it was empty or possibly there really was a bullet in another chamber, maybe it was my punky lucky day! The journalist from The Sun, Bob Hart, was already looking to upgrade the story from a column item to a spread! The Stranglers were looking decidedly queasy and there was a general sense of nervousness. They were in too deep and they knew it, but what to do? As I knew from experience any sudden movement was dangerous! They spent the next 18 months extracting themselves from the various Hells Angels chapters that had taken over their security or attached themselves to the band. All seemed a long way from the Hope and Anchor."

In November The Stranglers were back close to the Hope and Anchor once again for the Front Row festival. The pub landlord, Fred Grainger had been so good to the boys in the past and they frequently repaid the service by playing small gigs for him at the "Grope and Wanker" (Hugh's nickname for the place), where as many people as possible crammed their selves inside to witness their heroes in closed surroundings. A great live recording exists of the band at this venue, one recorded at the end of November. Hugh is on particularly hilarious form, especially during the band's rendition of their live favourite, Tits. "On a massive swelling organ, Dave Greenfield!" "The demon of the semen, Jean Jacques Burnel on the bloody bass!" "Now I'm gonna give you a bit of psychedelic lead guitar, just like Paul McCartney and John McLaughlin and all those creeps do."

Their next single, in the aftermath of those two enormously successful albums, was called Five Minutes. Much harder than their previous singles, it was loud, aggressive, sinister and at times closer to heavy metal than punk. The inspiration for the lyrics came from JJ. He had been living in a flat with Wilko Johnson from Dr Feelgood and a girl called Suzy. One night, when JJ was out, the girl was raped by five black men who had broken into the house. An angered JJ in the song says through gritted teeth, "I just want to find those guys that's all!"

Although the song was a minor departure for the band, and was far from commercial, the popularity of The Stranglers ensured the song reached Number 11 on the UK charts. Sound wise it pre dates their nest album, the much darker material to follow.

They may have had an undeniable air of menace, but their popularity was undeniable; at the end of 1977 they topped the Melody Maker's annual reader's poll as Best New Group. JJ, in typically outrageous fashion, posed nude for an NME centre-spread, where they named him Stud of the Year! They had sold around 2 million records in their first year and played over 100 gigs, setting a new record by selling out The London Roundhouse five nights in a row. Not bad going.

AFTER PUNK

Alan Edwards told me, "And so ended Phase One of The Stranglers - exciting years, but everyone was living just a bit too fast. Something had to change. No more heroes, for a while at least."

Some people have said that nothing interesting and exciting has happened in music since punk; this is of course arguable. Some good bands have come and gone but there hasn't been a musical movement since that has shocked the nation. But punk rock was kind of dead by 1979, and new wave was beginning to take shape and expand into other genres; electronic, euro pop, ska, the wave of hardcore punk. It was the beginning of a new and very fruitful period in The Stranglers world, where the music grew much more experimental and the tensions within the band began to shake their lives. Martin Rushent stayed on board to produce the band's third album, Black and White, but quit halfway through recording The Raven, by then finding their music too experimental and lacking great melody. Personally the band had not only become obnoxious, but totally unmanageable. Ian Grant said, "They were doing heroin and were unmanageable. I was constantly thwarted and frustrated." For many the quality of the band's musical output gradually declined after the 1970s. Although The Raven is a big fan favourite, I don't rate it as highly as the first three albums. Even Hugh Cornwell once said, "A lot of the very early stuff really took me away. Some of the later stuff was difficult to listen to. A lot of it didn't gel. The earlier stuff had a great sound that wasn't captured later on."

By The Raven, their musical style had almost turned to prog rock and it was clear drugs were having an effect on the music. They had also become paranoid and obsessed with UFOs and the mysterious Men in Black, a seldom seen clan of black clad men who apparently appear after a UFO sighting to silence the witnesses. So obsessed they did become with this dark subject in fact that they themselves began to constantly dress foot to head in black. They even wrote an album all about it, The Gospel According to the Meninblack; a dark, totally drugged up look into such murky areas as the second coming, alien abduction, manna, a rewritten version of the lord's prayer and haunting waltzes. Cornwell says drugs may have been a major part in the band's commercial down-slide. In 1980, Hugh wound up in prison for drug possession, missing a string of gigs at the Rainbow (in his absence they recruited a whole gang of new wave pals like Ian Dury, Wilko Johnson, Toyah, Hazel O Connor and funnily enough Phil Daniels.) A couple of months later the whole group were in prison after a riot at one of their gigs in Nice.

By the early 80s the band were a far less commercial draw than in the 70s, although they were still a considerably successful live act. Bad luck still followed them wherever they went; deaths in their close circle, all their gear getting stolen in the US. After the flop of the Meninblack album, UA had transformed into EMI and the label had little faith in The Stranglers. After over a year of disastrous and disturbing events, The Stranglers' luck changed when they finally put their men in black obsession behind them. After one more album, La Folie, and a career saving hit single, Golden Brown, the band left EMI to go to Epic Records. Before leaving, The Stranglers offered EMI a final single, the top 10 hit Strange Little Girl (ironically one of the demos UA had rejected in 1974) and the high selling Collection 77 – 82 album.

Cornwell eventually left in 1990 after getting bored of what he saw as the limitations the band's reputation put upon him and due to strains in his relationship with Burnel, who incidentally claims he and Hugh only had four arguments in their time in the band together. Hugh paints a different portrait, saying that the constant bickering got to him. Hugh wanted more from his creative life; he wanted to spread his wings and approach new horizons. But The Stranglers soldiered on without him, getting dropped from Epic Records upon Hugh's exit and going independent. They recruited singer Paul Roberts and guitarist John Ellis, releasing four mediocre albums in the 1990s and selling considerably less records than in their golden period. In 2000 Ellis left to be replaced by Baz Warne, former guitarist with Small-town Heroes. After the band's considerable comeback with the Norfolk Coast album in 2004, Roberts exited the band to pursue other goals. Warne took over vocal duties for the 2006 album, Suite 16, and continues to front the band. Sadly, Dave Greenfield passed away in 2020 of COVID, and Jet Black has left the band for good. Still, they continue to play live and release new music.

The story of the Stranglers is such a long, rich and varied one and I did not aim to tell it all here. They have dipped into almost every genre in their time; early techno, soft rock, pop, euro pop, soul, you name it. But I wanted to capture an era, a mood, an exciting time in music. I also had the urge to applaud a truly great rock n roll band.....the weird world of The Stranglers. I hope I succeeded and explained why The Stranglers reputation so often surpassed them. I also hope that the reader may understand the band's actions a little more now and accept them as an essential part of the punk story, even if Jon Savage insists on deleting them from it. They were the biggest and the best of their era, hands down. This book pretty much shows that. It is arguable whether the Stranglers would have made it at all had it not been for the revolutionary force that was punk rock. But this is a very small part of a rich legacy that still goes on to this day, against all odds.

May their music live on..........

CM-89
★あんまりニコニコするなよ
"BLIND"になっちまうぜ
SOMETIMES
サムタイムズ
the stranglers
ザ・ストラングラーズ
GO BUDDY GO
ゴー・バディ・ゴー
45r.p.m.
STEREO
¥600

ABOUT CHRIS WADE

Chris Wade is a UK based writer, filmmaker and musician. As well as running the acclaimed music project Dodson and Fogg, he has written books on Federico Fellini, Marlene Dietrich, Pablo Picasso, Marcello Mastroianni, Bob Dylan and many others. For his book on James Woods' film career, he interviewed the iconic actor for months. He has also released audiobooks of his comedic fiction, such as Cutey and the Sofaguard, narrated by Rik Mayall. He often records music with Nigel Planer, and runs a cult movie magazine called Scenes. For his varied projects he has interviewed such people as Sharon Stone, Stacy Keach, Oliver Stone, Jeff Bridges, Catherine Deneuve, Stephen Frears, Henry Jaglom and Bertrand Blier. His art films include The Apple Picker (winner of Best Film at Sydney World Film Festival), and he has made documentaries on such figures as Charlie Chaplin, Ken Russell, Orson Welles and George Melly, which have been shown on TV, had theatrical screenings, and are available on various streaming services as well as on DVD.

More info at his website: wisdomtwinsbooks.weebly.com

Printed in Great Britain
by Amazon